BEACON

CW00369968

long haul
check-in
in transit
jet lag
Flying
speed air rage
economy class sickness

Serge Barret
Thierry Lamiraud

CASSELL&CO

200,000

 58

the number of

people in flight at any one time.

2,200 km/h

(1,360 mph): the cruising speed of Concorde.

▶ 67

The more expensive your ticket, the more miles you earn. But miles are also awarded according to the distance travelled.

▶ 70

£7.5 billion

▶ 98 **This is the projected value of plane tickets to be sold over the Internet in 2002.**

£8 billion

The annual value of the counterfeit goods trade in the UK. ▶ 81

Flight time: **12 seconds.** *Distance covered :* **14 metres (46 ft).**

The first flight by the 'Flyer', the Wright brothers' biplane, on 17 December 1903. ▶ 12

2 billion passengers worldwide in the year 2000. ▶ 58

There are more than **300** *airlines operating in the world.* ▶ 68

The plane has become the ambassador of 'authentic' cuisines

Cajun prawns on the American Airlines flight to New Orleans;
Creole black pudding en route to the Caribbean with
Sabena, or Indian curry on the way to Bombay
with British Airways.

102

Cabin staff receive training lasting from 10 to 12 weeks to learn a job that calls for patience and efficiency.

84

In May 1930 Ellen Church invented the job that generations of girls were to dream of: air hostess.

▶ 19

'Low-cost' airlines cut their services to a minimum. They operate mainly out of Great Britain, Ireland and the Benelux countries.

▶ 69

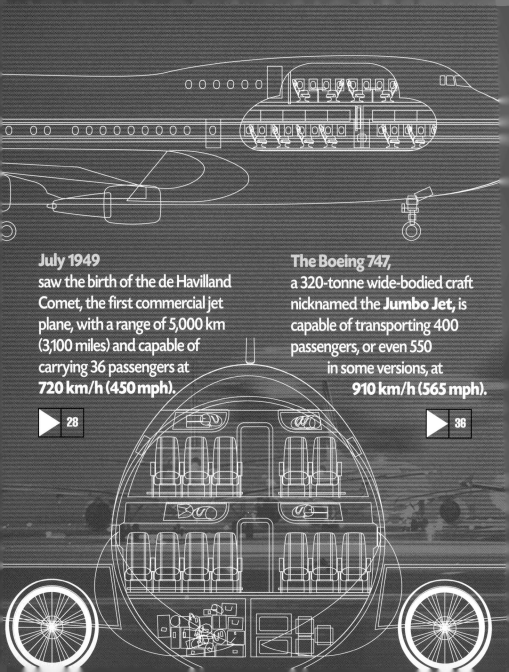

July 1949
saw the birth of the de Havilland Comet, the first commercial jet plane, with a range of 5,000 km (3,100 miles) and capable of carrying 36 passengers at **720 km/h (450 mph).**

▶ 28

The Boeing 747,
a 320-tonne wide-bodied craft nicknamed the **Jumbo Jet,** is capable of transporting 400 passengers, or even 550 in some versions, at **910 km/h (565 mph).**

▶ 36

21 January 1976 saw the joint inauguration
of the first commercial flights of Concorde:
the French set off to Rio de Janeiro,
while the British flew to Bahrain.

▶ 35

▶ 110 **The A3XX/A380, the plane of
the future, defies the laws of
aerodynamics to transport 650
passengers a distance of 16,000 km
(10,000 miles) in maximum comfort.
The craft weighs in at no less than
586 tonnes, and measures 80 m
(260 ft) both in diameter
and length.**

AIR FRANCE

70 minutes

the time it takes to get from the centre of Rome to Fiumicino airport

 78

IN EUROPE 1 FLIGHT IN 3 DEPARTS MORE THAN

 115

15 minutes late

For some people

the mere idea of flying in a plane
causes a panic attack that roots them
to the spot on terra firma.
This is quite a handicap, so airlines
are helping them to overcome their phobia
by offering 'fear-of-flying' courses.

Jet propulsion *became commonplace in the second half of the twentieth century. It was to revolutionise* **the design of airports** *and radically change their appearance. They were built further from towns and were* **bigger, more independent and more functional.**

 22

The use of mobile phones
or CD players is forbidden during take-off and landing.

 96

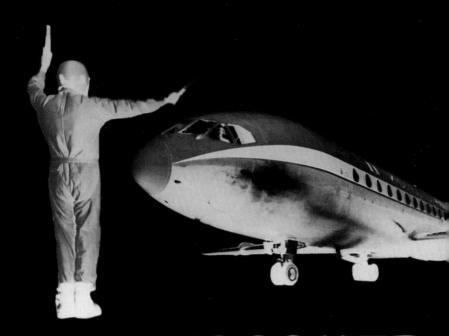

DISCOVER

THE DEVELOPMENT OF THE AEROPLANE WAS ONE OF THE GREAT ADVENTURE
STORIES OF THE 20TH CENTURY. ECONOMIC GROWTH AND TECHNOLOGICAL
ADVANCES HAVE MADE THE WORLD EVER SMALLER. AIR TRAVEL
FOR PASSENGERS STARTED TO EXPAND IN THE 1920S BUT BECAME WIDELY
AVAILABLE ONLY AT THE END OF THE 1960S. NOW THE CHALLENGE FOR
PASSENGER AVIATION IN THE NEW MILLENNIUM IS TO MARRY
THE AIMS OF PROFITABILITY WITH QUALITY OF SERVICE,
WHILE FULFILLING THE TRAVELLERS'
DREAMS OF ESCAPE ...

The place, Kitty Hawk, North Carolina, the United States; the date, 17 December 1903; the occasion, the Wright brothers' biplane, *Flyer*, slithers along the improvised runway between the dunes. It's a beautiful machine, constructed of canvas and wood, a sort of kite with an engine that backfires and splutters, bearing down on the skates that take the place of wheels. The *Flyer* vibrates, raising its nose rhythmically, and finally lifts itself awkwardly from the ground. Flight time: 12 seconds; distance covered: 14 metres (46 ft). There were several more attempts that day; on the fourth attempt they covered 284 metres (930 ft) at an altitude of 5 metres (16 ft). Not a lot, but enough to earn it a place in history as the first aeroplane flight. Most experts agree on this, relegating the performance of the Frenchman Clément Ader and his steam-powered 'bat' to the category of a mere 'jump'. Throughout the Edwardian era not a year went by without a record being broken or without further innovations. The list is long and the French were foremost: the first helicopter flight by Paul Cornu in Lisieux on 13 November 1907; the crossing of the Channel in 37 minutes by Louis Blériot on 25 July 1909; the flight of the first seaplane, constructed by Henri Fabre, on 28 March 1910 near Marseilles; the first crossing of the Mediterranean by Roland Garros on 23 September 1913.

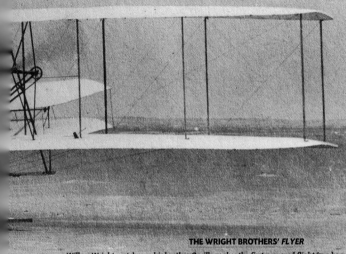

THE WRIGHT BROTHERS' *FLYER*
Wilbur Wright watches as his brother Orville makes the first powered flight in a heavier-than-air machine on 17 December 1903. In return, it was Wilbur who flew the first round trip in September 1904.

AIRSHIPS, PIONEERS OF AIR TRAVEL

The 'air aces', as they were called, were unwittingly writing the first lines in the history of commercial aviation, but they had some competition from the no less impressive airships, including those of Transaérienne, for example, the French company created on 2 March 1909, which claimed to provide 'any air travel service' but really just took passengers up for a ride in the gondola of an airship for fun. In the five years leading up to the First World War Transaérienne carried nearly 7,000 people from places as far apart as Reims, Nancy, Pau, Lucerne and Brussels. Between 1910 and 1914 the German company Delag flew 34,028 passengers, and the Zeppelin-built LZ.10 alone flew 3,622 passengers in 1911 and 1912.

Britain and American were surprisingly backward in airship travel. It was the Germans who undisputedly ruled the skies following the visionary dreams of their eccentric countryman Ferdinand von Zeppelin, who back in 1874 drew up sketches of the first giant airship. The gas was no longer held in one single soft pocket as had previously been the case but was distributed among several containers, which were arranged around the inside of a gigantic canvas cover.

GRAF ZEPPELIN

FRIEDRICHSHAFEN

BARCELONA

SEVILLA

PERNAMBUCO

RIO DE JANEIRO

BUENOS AIRES

L'AMÉRIQUE DU SUD
EN 3 JOURS

IN WAR OR PEACE AIRSHIPS RULED THE SKIES

The first Zeppelin was tested in 1900 over Lake Constance. Commercial success came in the summer of 1911, with the Zeppelin LZ-10 Schwaben, which completed a hundred flights without incident. With its mahogany furniture and mother-of-pearl inlays, the passenger cabin bore a strong resemblance to the great luxury trains of the time. On board, gracious living was the order of the day. It was only a cold menu, of course, but when that menu included limitless caviar and foie gras washed down by best vintage wines, nobody complained too much.

Then came the First World War, when the German airships were turned into bombers and the old Baron Zeppelin's little company became a flourishing industrial firm that, in the closing years of the conflict, was able to produce as many as two airships a month. After the capitulation of Germany in November 1918 the airships were seized and redistributed around France, Germany, Italy, Belgium and Japan.

High-performance airships were introduced at the end of the 1920s, making possible the first transatlantic crossings and epic journeys such as that of the *Graf Zeppelin*, which flew around the world in August 1929, carrying twenty passengers, all enjoying a luxury lifestyle. There was dancing on board, people dined in evening dress, chatted in the smoking room or on the promenade decks and later retired to private cabins. Unfortunately, the first tragic accidents followed soon after. One involved the English R-101, 236 metres (770 ft) of hydrogen-filled canvas, which came to grief near Beauvais on 5 October 1930 after a storm in the Channel, leaving 48 dead. Another involved the *Hindenburg*, which, on 6 May 1937, after crossing the Atlantic at a cruising speed of 130 km/h (130 mph), caught fire on its arrival at the Naval Air Station, Lakehurst, New Jersey. Miraculously, only 36 died. The disaster was watched by a radio reporter whose shocked account ran: 'It's burning, bursting into flames ... 'This is the worst of the worst catastrophes in the world ... 'four or five hundred feet into the sky ... 'Oh the humanity and all the passengers'. The catastrophe sent shock waves as deep as those caused by the sinking of the *Titanic* in 1912 and brought to an end the career of these giants of the sky, which were by now already considered too slow, to be superseded by more conventional aircraft. Until the disaster the *Hindenburg* had made ten round trips across the Atlantic and had carried more than a thousand passengers.

THE ZEPPELIN
Airships became very popular in a short space of time, but it was back to the drawing board after terrible accidents such as that suffered by the Hindenburg *on 6 May 1937.*

THOSE MAGNIFICENT MEN IN THEIR FLYING MACHINES

By the end of the First World War, Britain had 22,000 planes, Germany 15,000 and France 12,000 – enough aircraft for the first great airline companies, which in 1919 made some very draughty débuts using converted bombers capable of carrying four or five passengers, each of whom was very carefully weighed before take-off, a bizarre scenario to modern eyes, but the aircraft were less than robust and it was vital to establish the exact weight of the luggage and the passengers and to spread it evenly throughout the cabin. Gloves and sometimes heavy-duty goggles were worn by both passengers and crew as the flight was so uncomfortable. Everything creaked and shook, starting with the wicker seats, which groaned with the slightest movement. The noise of the engines was deafening, icy draughts cut through clothing, and oil leaks were a regular hazard ... Sometimes clods of mud would fly into the cabin on take-off. The pilots, exposed to the elements, flew by the seats of their pants, following railway lines, roads and waterways and reading the names of villages painted on the roofs of houses. Technical faults and bad weather meant that forced landings were not uncommon.

FLYING BECOMES COMMERCIAL

Sensing great commercial possibilities, designers threw their efforts into increasing the capacity of the planes. In 1919 the Farman Goliath appeared, a French aircraft that could transport up to a dozen passengers. More attention began to be paid to the comfort of the 'customers' and buildings for their use were built beside the runways. The first airport equipped with a radio was built in Croydon, near London, and an early form of control tower was built at Le Bourget, near Paris. Very soon air links were established between Britain, France, Belgium and Germany. In 1920 6,748 passengers passed through Le Bourget, compared to 978 in 1919.

On the business side, competition was beginning to hot up. As the market busily responded to demand, companies were launched, competed, formed partnerships or merged ... The years 1919 to 1923 saw the appearance of KLM in the Netherlands, Sabena in Belgium, Qantas in Australia and Scadt in Colombia. In Britain British Marine, Daimler, Instone and Handley-Page Transport started in 1919 and became the four constituent companies of Imperial Airways, which was formed on 1 April 1924. Between 1926 and 1927 came Lufthansa in Germany, Pan American Airways in the United States, Dobrolet (the beginnings of the future Aeroflot) in the Soviet Union and Varig in Brazil.

FARMAN, 1926

The Farman brothers, aviators, trainers and aircraft designers, founded one of the first airline companies open to passengers in 1919.

Technical progress led to the first intercontinental connections, which were achieved through short hops and stops, changing aircraft, or even company, *en route*. In May 1930 the French aviator Jean Mermoz established the first airmail link between Paris and Brazil. The main area of activity was Europe and its colonies, however. London thus became linked to the Cape in South Africa, to Brisbane in Australia and to the cities of India; Amsterdam was linked to Batavia in Indonesia, and Paris to Saigon. The trips were long, uncomfortable and exhausting. At the end of the 1930s it took ten and a half days on Air Orient to cover the 12,000 km (7,500 miles) between Paris and Saigon. Everything was included in the ticket price, which was astronomic: £1,800 at the time (about £4,000 today) ... Only the very best would do for the travelling elite, including the smartest hotels in the world.

AN IN-FLIGHT REVOLUTION: THE FIRST AIR HOSTESSES

The greatest innovation of the time, however, happened in the United States. It took the form of a nurse, Ellen Church, who in May 1930 managed to persuade the owner of Boeing Air Transport (United Airlines) of the benefits of a calming feminine presence on board. It was an immediate success: seven other nurses were taken on for the San Francisco to Chicago route. The idea swiftly crossed the Atlantic and arrived in Europe via Swissair.

Little by little, the idea of comfort crept into the hitherto rather masculine world of aviation, particularly on the Paris to London route, where LO-213s of the French service *Rayon d'or* as well as Handley Pages and other British Short Scyllas transported spellbound passengers across the Channel. Some planes were transformed into flying restaurants, and a *maître d'hôtel* would offer five- or six-course meals. Out of the windows (no portholes yet) passengers could compare bird's-eye views of the French and English countryside. These aircraft were high in comfort, but low in aerodynamics, being basically still variants on the original models of canvas and wood. Aircraft increased noticeably in size, but this was only to make more room for passengers, although it was still not possible to carry more than a handful of people. In 1926 the Fokker F-VII from the Netherlands flew at 190 km/h (120 mph) and carried eight passengers, and in the United States the Ford 4 AT Trimotor carried 14 passengers at 170 km/h (105 mph). However, it wasn't until 1933, with the arrival of a new type of aeroplane, the Boeing 247, that aviation really entered the age of comfort and speed.

ELLEN CHURCH, THE FIRST AIR HOSTESS
She invented the job generations of girls were to dream of ...

It was United Airlines in the United States that set the ball rolling with its exclusive use of the famous B-247. A metallic monoplane, it accommodated ten passengers in a soundproof, air-conditioned cabin and cruised at a speed of 250 km/h (155 mph). Transcontinental and Western

Air (TWA) immediately responded by putting into service the bigger and more comfortable DC-1, which was manufactured by Douglas, and very quickly followed by the DC-2, which could carry 14 passengers. The plane flew at 175 km/h (110 mph) and was fitted with deep-pile carpet, soft seats and eye-catching curtains. Was this all a build-up to the arrival in 1935 of the legendary DC-3, which could carry 21 passengers at 290 km/h (180 mph)? Some 10,000 of these planes were sold, a record in the history of aviation. In reply, Boeing designed the Stratoliner, a craft that flew at 400 km/h (250 mph) and carried 33 passengers. Unfortunately, the Stratoliner missed its début because of the Second World War ...

ON BOARD A PLANE, 1936

The interior of a plane belonging to a major commercial airline, probably a DC-3, identifiable by the shape of the portholes.

In Europe Lufthansa's Junkers 52 aircraft were considered by far the finest aircraft. They flew at nearly 300 km/h (185 mph) and could take 17 people. Including military production, nearly 4,800 of these craft were built.

LONG-DISTANCE ROUTES AND THE RISE OF THE SEAPLANE

In spite of their capabilities, none of these craft could travel very long distances, and certainly not across the Atlantic. Hence the idea of a plane that could 'land' in any patch of calm water and refuel or put down in the sea in case of breakdown. So the seaplane, with its wide fuselage inspired by the hull of a boat – a real flying palace, as luxurious as the airships, or, on a larger scale, the great liners – came into being.

In the 1930s people were on the move, not only on land and by sea, but also in the air, between the Old World and its colonies. Britain had its sights set on the skies of Africa and India, France looked towards Africa and the Far East, but France had lost its lead in the field of aviation. Its Bréguets, CAMS, Liorés and Oliviers were quickly overtaken. Dramatic events in the shape of the Second World War intervened, and the final test flight of the giant seaplane Latécoère 521, intended to provide a regular service over the North Atlantic in September 1939, took place just five days before the declaration of war.

The British, on the other hand, were using tri-engined seaplanes with a hull that could carry 15 people, going by the splendid name of Short Calcutta. They were slow – (145 km/h (90 mph) – but had a well-deserved reputation for safety. In 1931 they were joined by the Short Kent, a quadri-engined seaplane that could carry 16 passengers.

The Americans were content to concentrate on the Caribbean, Latin America, Australia, New Zealand and China using three craft: the Sikorsky 42, (at 300 km/h (185 mph), the Martin 130, which came into service in 1934, and the Boeing 314 Clipper, launched in 1938. It was this last model that flew the first regular route opened up by Pan Am between the United States and Europe. It linked New York to Marseilles and Southampton via the Azores, Bermuda and Lisbon.

The use of seaplanes to cover very long distances and the need for numerous stop-overs led to aerodromes being built near to the coasts. Amsterdam, Barcelona, Copenhagen, Lisbon, Los Angeles, New York and Rome were to become the most used.

FROM BUMPY FIELDS TO RUNWAYS, OBSERVATION TERRACES, RESTAURANTS AND BARS: AIRPORTS COME OF AGE

Old landing strips, which had appeared here and there as need arose, were coping less and less well with the demands placed upon them. They were often nothing more than flat grassy areas or fields without marked-out runways, and planes took off into whichever direction the wind happened to be coming from. The passenger facilities, where they existed, were not much different from the aircraft hangars. No one thought of complaining much, as these rather spartan arrangements were nevertheless part of aviation's general air of glamour. This was the case until 1928, when New York was stirred with excitement at the opening of Newark, the first modern airport worthy of the name: it had a surfaced runway, passengers no longer had to wade through mud to get to the aircraft, and the reception buildings were the forerunners of airport terminals as we know them today.

The capitals and great cities of the world followed suit and began to build airports away from their centres. Road and rail links were built to improve access, runways were lit, radio links were established, and administrative and customs facilities were expanded. Passengers could now enjoy the facilities of waiting rooms, observation terraces, restaurants, bars with panoramic views ... These new airports became imbued with a sort of magic that until then had only been found in the ports or great railway stations.

A DESIGN FOR AN AIRPORT

A display at the 1939 World's Fair in New York.

People came from far and wide just to see the planes take off and envied those modern-day adventurers who in a matter of hours would be miles away in exotic parts of the world. On Sundays Londoners would make an excursion to Croydon, Parisians went to Le Bourget, Berliners to Tempelhof and Amsterdamers to Schiphol.

The number of passengers continued to grow. In the United States, where there had been 200,000 passengers in 1929, there were 2 million in 1939. During the same period Europe saw the total number of passengers increase from 180,000 to 800,000.

It wasn't until after the war, however, that airline travel became really established and really made its mark in the history of transport.

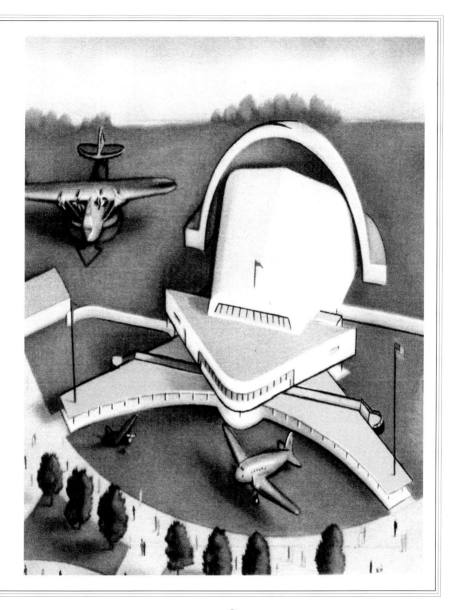

THE FIRST PRESSURISED CABIN

After the Second World War, as had been the case at the beginning of the 1920s, some military craft were modified to turn them into commercial aeroplanes. The British Lancaster bomber was transformed into the Lancastrian, and the Lockheed C-69 was converted into the Constellation. The reliable Boeing 377 Stratocruiser, based on the B-29 Superfortress, went into service, and the trials of pressurised cabins continued in the wake of those that had been conducted on the Boeing 307 Stratoliner. Its passenger cabin, which was completely sealed, took in compressed air, which allowed the ambient pressure at 2,500 metres (8,000 ft) to be maintained at very high altitude. Suddenly the plane could fly a lot faster, because the air, being much lighter high up, offers less resistance. In addition, their cruising altitude, well above any storm clouds, spared passengers the discomfort of rollercoaster plane rides, and to accommodate its passengers even more comfortably, Boeing developed a seat that would suit 'a 7-stone blonde as easily as a big 16-stone man'. In spite of this, only 55 Stratocruisers were sold, and the plane is famous today as much for the glamour of the bar installed on its lower deck as for its technical capabilities.

POLITICS COME INTO PLAY

After the war, civilian life quickly returned to normal. Industry used what it had learned during the conflict to speed up the construction of aircraft and developed planes specifically for commercial aviation. This led to the introduction of the DC-6, the Convair 440, the Lockheed Electra and the Ilyushin 18. The number of air passengers grew spectacularly from 4 million in 1941 to 6 million in 1945. Companies flourished almost everywhere. BOAC (British Overseas Airways Corporation) took over the routes of Imperial Airways, and Air France, its services suspended during the war, resumed operations in 1945. Similarly with Sabena, KLM, Qantas and Air Canada. The 1940s also saw new or newly independent countries founding their own airlines.

DOUGLAS DC-6

Specially designed for commercial flights at the end of the Second World War.

The boom in air travel began as soon as the war ended. In order to avoid chaos, the Allies met in Chicago in November 1944 and signed an international agreement recognising the control of each sovereign state over its airspace. In 1946, in a meeting on the Atlantic islands of Bermuda, the Americans and the British agreed to institute a charter introducing the basic principle that was to govern the whole of post-war commercial air transport. This charter was chiefly concerned with states' control over the prices charged by the airlines serving them. In other words, a direct attack on free competition and a huge brake on what could have been the

beginnings of a noticeable fall in ticket prices. The 'democratisation of the skies' was hardly at the top of the agenda.

However, at shop-floor level the real debate concerned the engine. Should the plane be powered by a turboprop or a turbojet? Should the designers stick to a combination of propeller and gas turbine or take a leap into the dark with jet propulsion? The airlines dithered, wary of innovation, and played safe. Thus the years 1950 to 1959 saw the entry into service of 440 turboprop craft, more or less elongated versions of the British Vickers Viscount 700, throughout most of the world. Its final version, the V-810, could carry 75 passengers at 580 km/h (360 mph).

ENTERING THE JET AGE

As far back as 1930, Frank Whittle, a bright young cadet at the Royal Air Force College in Cranwell, had patented an idea for a jet engine. According to him, this invention would allow for flight speeds of nearly 800 km/h (500 mph), at altitudes where the air is much less dense than at sea level. The only problem was finding materials that could resist the high temperatures of the jet engines. It wasn't easy, but he was driven by a youthful determination, and on 12 April 1937 his jet engine, the first of its kind, was ready. His triumph was tempered by a bitter disappointment because Whittle was finally pipped to the post by Pabst von Ohain. This young German had been working on an identical project and enjoyed considerable moral, material and financial support. As a result, on 27 August 1939 he became the first to equip a jet plane to fly.

From then on, competition was fierce, and on 15 May 1941 the Gloster E-28/39, the first English plane to have a Whittle W-1 engine, took off. It flew nearly as fast as the best military craft even though it had only half their power. Another turbojet was then added to enhance its capabilities, taking the craft's speed to 745 km/h (460 mph), and the jet age began in earnest. Unfortunately, the war and the agreements made with the United States were of no help to British civil aviation, which was neglected during this period. The Americans continued making commercial aircraft, which they then sold to the Europeans, who were devoting their own energies to military aviation. This led to a situation in 1945 where there was not a single high-performance British plane to match the DC-4 and other American Constellations.

THE JET ENGINES OF A BOEING 747

The Boeing 747 flew for the first time in 1969. At that time it was the aircraft of superlatives: the biggest, it could travel the furthest and carry the most passengers.

The two national British companies, BOAC and BEA, had to make do with aircraft produced across the Atlantic to equip their fleets. Until such time, that is, that they decided to draw on their own resources and began to exploit the formidable technical advances made as part of the war effort.

July 1949 saw the birth of the de Havilland Comet, the first commercial jet plane, which had a range of 5,000 km (3,000 miles) and was capable of carrying 36 passengers at 720 km/h (450 mph). It was an innovation that infuriated the Americans: 'The British are giving the Americans a run for their money in jet flight,' ran the specialist press. Thousands of spectators at London airport applauded the take-off of the Comet's first commercial flight to Rome. The Americans were enraged, casting doubt over the safety of the craft, but to no avail. The jet engines had halved the journey time, BOAC flights were fully booked, and de Havilland's order books were full. Air France was the first to be interested in the new plane, followed by UTA (Unions de Transport Aériens), Canadian Pacific, the Australians, the Brazilians, the Japanese and finally ... Pan Am. Everything seemed to be going so well for British aviation. Until the dreadful day of 2 May 1953 when farmers near Calcutta suddenly saw the remains of an aeroplane, plummeting down from the sky. The world was stunned and doubts about the techni-cal reliability of the plane were raised. It was decided that the acci-dent, which left 43 people dead, could not be attributed to human error, which had been believed to be the case in the previous crashes involving Comets taking off from Rome on 26 October 1952 and from Karachi on 3 March 1953. Unfortunately the grim toll was far from complete. Eight months later, on 10 January 1954, the pilot of the Comet *Yoke Peter*, which had just left Rome to fly to London radioed the pilot of another plane, an Argonaut flying a little lower than himself 'Have you received my mess ...'. And then nothing, just a crackling radio. The pilot of the Argonaut knew instantly: the Comet had fallen. In London, there was great consterna-tion. Wild theories flew around, and there was talk of a bomb or even a terrorist plot ...

PASSENGERS ON BOARD THE COMET

In the 1950s passenger comfort got a little more up to date. However, it was still aimed at an elite market.

De Havilland's Comet in action, December 1949.

COMET FLIGHTS SUSPENDED

All kinds of theories were put forward to explain the accidents, until finally serious reservations were expressed about the premature wear of the metal of the cabin due to pressurization. While awaiting the results of the enquiry, Miles Thomas, president of BOAC, suspended the flights of his Comet aircraft. Scattered debris of *Yoke Peter* was recovered from the sea off the islands of Elba and Monte Cristo, and the flight instruments were found intact. Searches and tests were made, but nothing significant was found. So, at the end of March, and without even waiting for the end of the investigations, the Comet went back into service, although it was made clear that some 50 different modifications had been made.

THE COMET, 1952

This legendary plane was the jewel in the crown of British aviation, until it was involved in several mysterious accidents.

Some days later, on 8 April 1954, the editorial offices of the world's press were in ferment. All evening, teleprinters were busy reporting the disappearance of yet another Comet somewhere between Rome and Cairo. As before, the craft exploded in flight. This was one too many. The Air Registration Board withdrew the Comet I's certificate of airworthiness and Winston Churchill himself declared that 'The cost of solving the Comet mystery must be reckoned neither in money nor in manpower'.

The dreadful cause was finally established. With the help of models and dummies, the final moments of the craft were re-created. The reconstructions showed that in a split second a slight crack in the pressurised cabin had created an overwhelming out-draught in which seats and passengers would have been mercilessly thrown around the cabin. The tests and reconstructions that had been filmed revealed that the successive accidents happening to the Comet were due to a decompressive explosion resulting from the weakness of the porthole frames. So the metal structure of the aircraft itself had been to blame, not human error.

THE TRIUMPH OF THE BOEING 707

De Havilland set about making improvements to the Comet, sparing no expense or effort. The result was that on 4 October 1958 a new version of the Comet IV completed its maiden flight between London and New York, stopping to refuel in Newfoundland. However, the new Comet caused little stir because by now the press were much more interested in the reconnaissance flight of Pan Am's Boeing 707, which took place at the same time. It seemed as if the Americans had been able to draw lessons from the Comet's misfortune. They thus took advantage of De Havilland's four-year absence to build the Boeing 707 in record time. A stronger and more spacious craft, with a longer range than the Comet, it was at the cutting edge of technology,

halving flying times and attracting all the major airline companies. Not content with this success, the Americans twisted the knife when at the same time they brought out a DC-8, a four-
engined jet capable of carrying between 115 and 175 passengers, depending on the model, at a
speed of 900 km/h (560 mph) over a distance of 1,000 km (620 miles).

THE CARAVELLE: A JEWEL IN THE FRENCH CROWN

The French were stung into a response, and, in 1959, under the badge of Air France, they put into
service the Caravelle, with a range of 1,600 km (990 miles) and flying at 780 km/h (480 mph).
It could carry between 64 and 99 passengers and had two jet engines at each side of the fuselage. The Caravelle won much praise, and people marvelled at its silent engines. The press
reported on experiments in which it had glided without any mechanical assistance from Paris
to Dijon. Throughout its time in service the Caravelle was to prove to be the plane that had the
fewest accidents. It was also one of the most heavily copied, not least by the DC-9, a medium-
haul American plane, of which 900 were built, three times as many as the Caravelle.
As jet propulsion became commonplace in the second half of the 20th century, it transformed the design of airports and radically changed their appearance. They were built
further away from towns and became bigger, more independent and more
functional. A system of walkways was introduced against which the
aeroplanes could draw up, so that passengers would not have to
move around the runways. Hotels and business centres

THE CARAVELLE, 1959
*This French plane was much admired for
its technical features as well as its
comfort and reliability.*

were built near by, duty-free shops were expanded, and avant-garde architecture was commissioned. This was the time when Dulles opened in Washington, when the famous TWA terminal was built in New York, when Heathrow in London was added to Gatwick, when Schiphol was extended in Amsterdam and Orly was built in Paris. The great capital cities had to respond to the demands of the 'jet revolution', beginning with the increase in the number of passengers, which, thanks to a combination of more flights and bigger planes, had grown from 20.3 million in 1949 to 141 million by 1965.

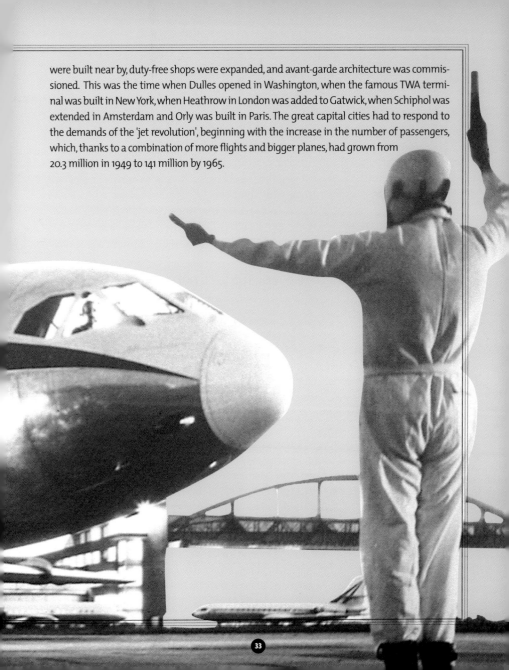

CONCORDE: FROM DREAM TO DISAPPOINTMENT

It was in the ebullient atmosphere prevailing at the beginning of the 1960s that the idea of a supersonic commercial aircraft came about. The Russians made designs for the Tupolev 144, the Americans worked on the Boeing 2 707, and French and British engineers teamed up to design Concorde. In the end, only the Franco-British project stayed the course. And what a project! Emerging from the realm of dreams, it trailed a suitably romantic story of diplomatic incidents, scientific endeavour and cross-border compromise behind it. There were occasional near-disasters, and it was even believed that the project would not see completion. However, on 2 March 1969 the great bird completed its first flight in front of a crowd of journalists specially despatched to Toulouse-Blagnac airport in France. This first trial was a terrifically exciting moment in aviation history, foreshadowing its commercial entry into service, seven years and many disappointments later.

A BIG BIRD THAT FLEW TOO NEAR TO THE SUN ...

The validity of the Concorde project was called into question on environmental as well as economic grounds. It was alleged in some quarters that the problems were due to a move initiated by the Americans, who were anxious to protect their own aircraft industry. Concorde was criticised for anything and everything. It was accused of costing three times as much as anticipated, of using too much fuel, of causing more pollution than other jets, of being too noisy, of creating huge bangs as it broke the sound barrier, of making a hole in the ozone layer and even of causing pregnant women to miscarry and asphyxiating passengers through an excess of ozone ... The pressure was such that in 1971 the American government intimated that the plane might be unwelcome at some American airports, and in 1973 the US Senate

CONCORDE, 1969

Numerous false stories contributed to the mythology of the great white bird, the first supersonic project to come to fruition.

simply prohibited any civil aircraft from flying supersonically over American territory. Nearly every country followed the United States's lead, including France and Britain. The business world's response was swift: Pan Am, American Airlines, TWA, Air Canada and Iran Air all cancelled their orders. Other companies followed suit, and by the end of 1973 it was certain that Concorde would only fly under the Air France and British Airways insignia. Without the US market the future of the Franco-British supersonic plane seemed uncertain. Another market had to be found, and sights were set instead on South America, Africa, Asia and even Canada. On 21 January 1976 there was a joint inauguration of the first commercial flights: the French set off for Rio de Janeiro and the British flew to Bahrain. The 100 passengers on the

London-Bahrain flight covered the distance in 3 hours 38 minutes, whereas those flying from Paris arrived in Brazil in a little under 7 hours, including a stop in Dakar. Finally, following a change in policy by the American administration, Washington and New York airports agreed to take Concorde, in 1976 and 1977 respectively, but it was too late. The plane designed years earlier was now considered too fuel-hungry, and the routes served by the two companies were all losing money. Only the flights between Europe and New York were retained.

In the light of the disaster in Paris in 2000, when 113 people lost their lives, British Airways and Air France decided to ground their Concorde fleets. It looks as if it may be the end of the line for this Anglo-French partnership and this wonderful aircraft, although attempts to save it with a new safety plan involving armour for its fuel tanks and non-shredding tyres are being considered.

THE SUCCESS OF THE JUMBOS

At the end of the 1960s, at around the same time that Concorde was being developed, Boeing launched another, arguably more successful venture: the enormous Boeing 747, a 320-tonne wide-bodied craft affectionately known as the Jumbo Jet, capable of transporting 400 passengers, 550 in some versions, at 910 km/h (565 mph). With the introduction of this plane, Boeing was clearly putting its money on a future of mass transport, a complete change from the original elitist image of air transport. Companies throughout the world ordered the B-747 in great numbers. McDonnell Douglas and Lockheed followed in hot pursuit, and in the 1970s they introduced the DC-10 (380 passengers in a single class) and the TriStar (345 passengers). Having learned from their experience with Concorde, the European manufacturers finally realised that it would be better to unite in the face of the all-powerful Americans. In 1966 the aviation consortium Airbus Industrie, which included French, German, British and Spanish

THE NOSE OF A BOEING 747

Its passenger capacity of 400 and its cruising speed of more than 900 km/h (560 mph) met the needs of the age of mass transport.

designers, announced the construction of a medium-haul aircraft, the Airbus A-300, capable of carrying 300 passengers. The first of these planes was put into service in France, Germany and Spain in 1974, in an atmosphere of deep gloom. Some airlines, including Indian Airlines and South African Airlines, had bought the airbus, but numbers were far too low to call it a success. Then in 1977 Eastern Airlines ordered several Airbuses for its New York to Miami route, thus opening up the huge American market to the European plane. The A-310 programme was then launched at the same time as the first plans for the A-320 were drawn up. Later came the launches of the enormously successful A-330 and the A-340.

At the end of the Second World War, the annual number of passengers stood at 20.3 million. In 2002 it is expected to reach 317.18 million: a 15-fold increase! This huge expansion obviously owes much to technological advances, but, can also be explained by governments being willing to act to break up monopolies and open up air travel to competing market forces. Charter flights have now become commonplace, and low-cost services, where companies offer minimal in-flight service, but cheap tickets, have recently appeared on the air travel scene.

And who could object? Certainly not the consumer, who benefits from the fierce competition between the airlines. It is all down to who can go the fastest, the furthest and at the lowest price. Our shrinking world is accessible to an ever greater number of people. The statisticians forecast an increase in air traffic of 5 per cent a year until 2015, with a subsequent increase in demand for aircraft. It is probably the range of the largest jets carrying 240 to 400 passengers, which will see the highest demand. Technical innovations are orientated around this increase in traffic. Airlines demand ever safer and more fuel-efficient planes, with the profitability/passenger comfort ratio becoming ever more important. Quieter aircraft are planned, equipped with sophisticated equipment for passengers and the aviation world is excitedly following Airbus's A3XX/A380 project, not due for completion until 2004. This long-haul aircraft should be the biggest commercial plane in the skies, with a passenger capacity of between 550 and 800 passengers, accommodated on two decks, and offer various in-flight services, from sleeping cabins and shops to even a gym ... It will have a range of around 15,000 km (9,300 miles).

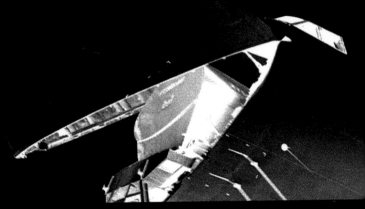

LOOK

AN AIRPORT AT NIGHT HAS THE MAGIC OF A FLOODLIT BALLET.
PILOTS PREPARE THEIR FLIGHTS DOWN TO THE LAST DETAIL, MAINTENANCE
STAFF MAKE METICULOUS TECHNICAL CHECKS, CARGO IS LOADED,
ALL BEFORE THE SLEEPY EYES OF THE PASSENGERS.
THE ROLE OF THE CONTROL TOWER IS CRUCIAL AS
SCORES OF PLANES TAKE OFF INTO THE NIGHT SKY.

The control tower.

Loading freight.

Loading cargo planes.

Loading luggage.

Sorting packages.

Apron gantry for boarding the planes.

Terminal 2F.

Pilots preparing for their flight.

Maintenance of the lights on runway 4.

Day breaks ...

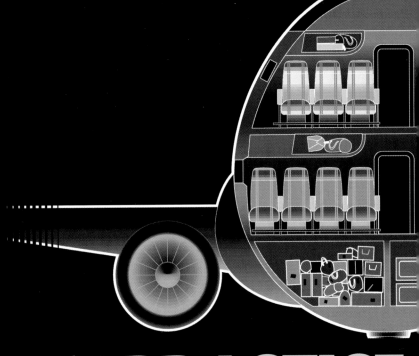

IN PRACTICE

HOW TO CHOOSE YOUR FLIGHT, HOW TO READ A TICKET.
WHERE TO SIT TO MINIMISE TURBULENCE. UNDERSTAND HOW A PLANE FLIES.
CUSTOM AND PASSPORT INFORMATION,
THE SECRETS OF STAYING WELL ON BOARD,
DIFFERENT TICKET TARIFFS
– THERE'S MORE TO AIR TRAVEL
THAN MEETS THE EYE.

What's going on in the skies?

Nearly 2 billion passengers travelled by plane in the year 2000, 100 times more than 50 years ago! It's been calculated that 200,000 people are in flight at any one time ... And yet in spite of this huge growth in numbers, flying has never been safer.

The top ten destinations in the world.
Figures for 1999, in millions of passengers

London (4 airports) : 103.6
New York (3 airports) : 92.6
Chicago (3 airports) : 86.3
Tokyo (2 airports) : 80
Atlanta (1 airport) : 78
Los Angeles (3 airports) : 70.8
Paris (2 airports) : 69
Dallas (2 airports) : 66.8
Frankfurt (1 airport) : 45.8
Houston (1 airport) : 42
Source : Aéroports magazine,1999.

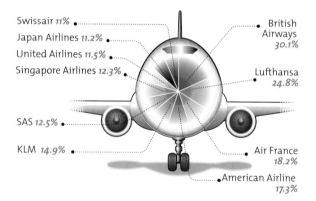

Swissair *11%*
Japan Airlines *11.2%*
United Airlines *11.5%*
Singapore Airlines *12.3%*
SAS *12.5%*
KLM *14.9%*
British Airways *30.1%*
Lufthansa *24.8%*
Air France *18.2%*
American Airline *17.3%*

THE TOP TEN AIRLINES
International flights only
– in millions of passengers

A RAPID INCREASE IN 50 YEARS

1950
21 million passengers

1975
318 million passengers

1995
1.4 billion passengers

2000
2 billion passengers (estimated)

THE WORLD'S BUSIEST ROUTES

Between the major zones
Within the major zones

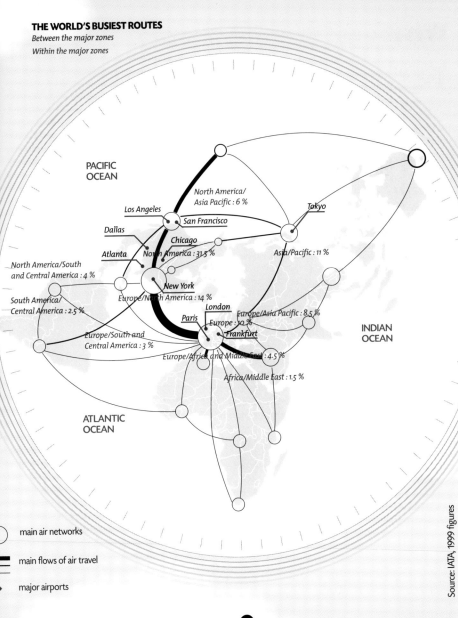

PACIFIC
OCEAN

North America/
Asia Pacific : 6 %

Los Angeles

Dallas

San Francisco

Chicago

Atlanta

North America : 31.5 %

Tokyo

Asia/Pacific : 11 %

North America/South
and Central America : 4 %

New York

South America/
Central America : 2.5 %

Europe/North America : 14 %

London

Paris

Europe/Asia Pacific : 8.5 %

Europe : 10 %

Europe/South and
Central America : 3 %

Frankfurt

Europe/Africa and Middle East : 4.5 %

INDIAN
OCEAN

Africa/Middle East : 1.5 %

ATLANTIC
OCEAN

main air networks

main flows of air travel

major airports

Source: IATA, 1999 figures

59

The routes through the sky

The sky is a highway just like a motorway. There are rush hours and traffic jams, but it is complicated by an additional difficulty: a plane cannot slow to a complete standstill ...

The motorways of the skies

The French, Swiss, Italian and German authorities introduced a new network in February 1999 to improve traffic flow in the skies over Europe. The 'motorways of the sky' are parallel tracks, one on top of the other, 600 metres (2,000 ft) apart in altitude. Planes at the same altitude always go in the same direction and have to stay 9.2 km (5 nautical miles) behind the one in front. This means that aircraft do not get near each other in flight and safety is guaranteed no matter how many planes are flying.

Approaching airports

Aerial traffic jams are a particular problem on the approach to airports because this is where the arrival and departure corridors converge. So-called 'road' maps have been drawn up with gyratory schemes, to reduce the problem of delays and to keep pace with the demand for air travel

Technology eases the traffic problem

Until relatively recently, planes had to follow beacons on the ground to find their way, which meant that large numbers of planes gathered in the same portion of air space. New technologies linked to navigation instruments, particularly GPS (Global Positioning Systems), allow the planes to find their way wherever they are.

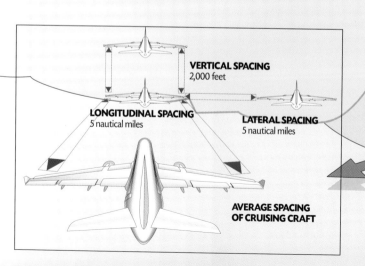

VERTICAL SPACING
2,000 feet

LONGITUDINAL SPACING
5 nautical miles

LATERAL SPACING
5 nautical miles

**AVERAGE SPACING
OF CRUISING CRAFT**

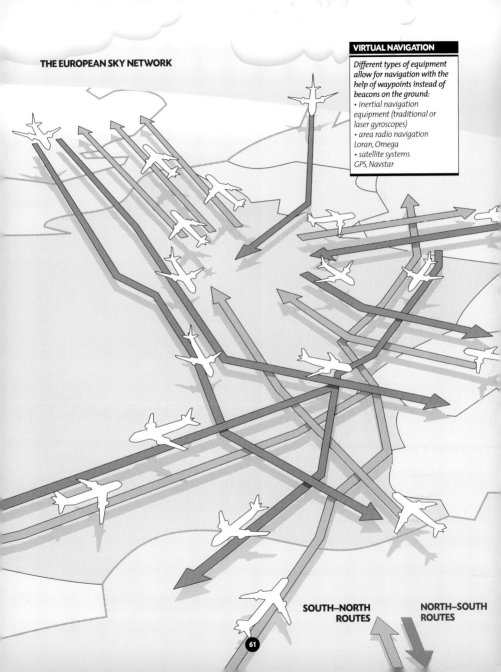

THE EUROPEAN SKY NETWORK

VIRTUAL NAVIGATION

Different types of equipment allow for navigation with the help of waypoints instead of beacons on the ground:
• *inertial navigation equipment (traditional or laser gyroscopes)*
• *area radio navigation Loran, Omega*
• *satellite systems GPS, Navstar*

SOUTH–NORTH ROUTES

NORTH–SOUTH ROUTES

What makes a plane fly?

They weigh several tens of thousands of tons ... and yet they fly! Where craft filled with air, such as balloons, airships and others, stay up in the air thanks to the Archimedean principle (like a boat in water), this principle is not applicable to conventional aircraft made of metal.

Drawing support from the air
A plane moves forwards thanks to its engines or its propellers, which create thrust; it is supported by the lift provided by the air when in motion. The flow of air, which circulates from the front to the back of the craft, is split when it meets a wing, then re-merged afterwards. The air stream travels further over the upper surface of the wing which is curved, than over the lower surface. The air moving over the top of the wing, is therefore going faster, forming an area of low pressure above the wing, which pulls upwards: this is called 'lift'.

'Wings' fly ...
Drag, caused by the friction of air on the wings, slowing the plane down, is lessened by the aerodynamic shape of the wings. On the lower surface of the wing, high pressure is exerted, two or three times weaker than the suction on the upper surface.

Taking off and landing
On landing and take-off, in order to compensate for slower speed, the surface area of the wing can be increased and more lift obtained by using mechanisms, such as the leading edge slats and the flaps. On take-off, the plane is nose up to increase the incidence – in other words, the angle of the wing to the air flow – increasing lift and facilitating take-off.

LIFT
It depends on four factors:
• the density of the air
• the surface of the wings
• the speed squared
• the shape and configuration of the wing.
The suction on the upper surface of the wing makes up two-thirds of the aerodynamic lift of the wing and the high pressure on the underside one-third.

LIFT

WEIGHT OF THE PLANE

THE SPEEDS FOR TAKE-OFF

• V1:
the critical speed below which take-off should be aborted should an engine fail; above this speed, the pilot should proceed with take-off. Usually, the aircraft mass is so great that it will not be able to land without jettisoning some of its fuel.

• V2:
the speed necessary for the plane to climb at the required rate after take-off.

• VR :
(meaning 'rotation speed'):
the speed at which the aeroplane can raise the nose up and take off safely.

• VLOF
(meaning 'lift-off speed'):
the speed at which the aircraft takes off. It follows on from Vr.

WING SECTIONS

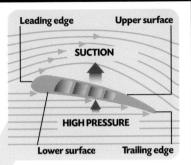

Leading edge   Upper surface

SUCTION

HIGH PRESSURE

Lower surface   Trailing edge

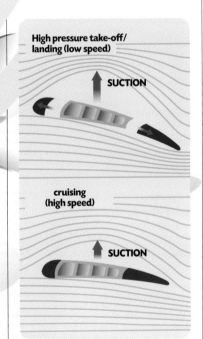

High pressure take-off/ landing (low speed)

SUCTION

cruising (high speed)

SUCTION

Servicing and maintenance

The maintenance of planes is carried out in several stages. The regular servicing of an airline's fleet is checked by independent organisations in some countries. A plane should always be in an 'as new' condition.

A test plane acts as a guinea pig for reputable airlines. It undergoes various tests to ascertain how a model is ageing. Routine servicing involves noting any problems that occur in flight and notifying the relevant airline safety organisation, which in the UK is the CAA. In addition, every 15 to 18 months there are tests on the controls and instrumentation, the landing gear, the engines and the general structure. Finally, every five years comes the 'major check-up': a complete overhaul in which the aeroplane is completely dismantled and checked, piece by piece.

STRUCTURE
Every 5,000 hours (or every 15 to 18 months) the fuselage and wings are examined to check that there are no cracks. Every ten years, the airframe is renovated.

AVIONIC SYSTEMS
These are the central controls for information and control of the aeroplane. Navigation, automatic pilot, flight controls, radio communication, warning panels, control screens and engines are constantly being inspected.
A complete check occurs every 15 to 18 months.

CAA (Civil Aviation Authority)
Engineers and experts in many different fields inspect all UK airline fleets. They issue Certificates of Airworthiness (C of A) and check that examinations of the craft and flight personnel are regularly carried out. Equipment reports, on which any in-flight technical incidents are recorded by the crew, are passed on to the organisation.

SRG (Safety Regulation Group)
Responsible for safety in civil aviation, this division of the CAA oversees crew training, aircraft maintenance, airline competence, airports and Air Traffic Control.

CPG (Consumer Protection Group)
This division of the CAA licences airlines and protects against dishonest travel agents. It also helps consumers when agents or airlines go bust.

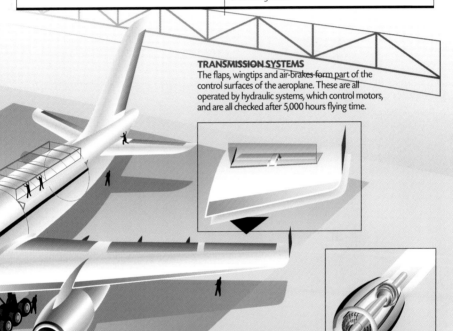

TRANSMISSION SYSTEMS
The flaps, wingtips and air-brakes form part of the control surfaces of the aeroplane. These are all operated by hydraulic systems, which control motors, and are all checked after 5,000 hours flying time.

LANDING GEAR
The tyres are replaced frequently, as they are subject to wear that is a thousand times heavier than car tyres. Brakes and legs are checked daily. Every 10,000 cycles (take-off and landing), the gear is completely overhauled.

ENGINES
With every generation the reliability and strength of jet engines improves tenfold. The engine is stripped down every 10,000 hours. The combustion chamber is reconditioned halfway through its life.

The types of craft

Boeing 747

With the exception of Concorde, which is in a category of its own, there are three main categories of craft among the hundreds of models in service. They may have fewer than ten seats or as many as 500, and they are suited to different types of trip.

Long-haul craft

These are used for long distances, often over 9,000 km (5,600 miles), and have a seating capacity from 240 to more than 500. This is the category in which aircraft designers are introducing most innovations. Most of the large craft are Boeing 777s, 767s, 747s (some having an upper deck) or Airbus A-340s or A-330s. McDonnell Douglas DC-10s and MD-11s, and Russian Ilyushin 62s also fall into the long-haul category.

Medium-haul craft

This range covers from long-haul to domestic use, from 2,500 to 5,000 km (1,500 to 3,000 miles), with a capacity of from 100 to 240 seats. They often have only two airclasses of ticket: economy and business. Airbus and Boeing dominate the market with the A-300, A-320, A-321 and the 727, 737, 757 models respectively; then there are also the DC-9 and MD-90 and the Tu 154.

'Commuter' planes

Normally restricted to 3,000 km (1,900 miles), these small craft often take fewer than 80 passengers in a single class. The most common are the Fokker or the Aerospatiale/Alenia ATR.

ATR-42
Length: 22.7 metres - Wingspan : 24.6 metres - No. of seats : 42 - Cruising speed : 550 km/h

747-100

Boeing 747-400

Fokker 100
Length : 35.53m - Wingspan : 28.08 metres - No. of seats : 103 - Cruising speed : 780 km/h

DC 9-81
Length : 32.86 m - Wingspan : 45.08 metres - No. of seats :130 - Cruising speed : 730 to 800 km/h

THE TYPICAL FLEET OF A NATIONAL CARRIER

Boeing 777-200 ER 11 craft
- Length : 63.70 metres - Wingspan : 60.93 metres
- No. of seats : 270 - Cruising speed : 900 km/h

Boeing 747- 400 13 craft
- Length : 70.67 metres - Wingspan : 64.94 metres
- No. of seats : 250/391 - Cruising speed : 990 km/h

Boeing 747- 300 /- 200 /- 100 26 craft
(15 passenger and 11 cargo)
- Length : 70.67 metres - Wingspan : 59.64 metres
- No. of seats : 239-508
- Maximum live load B747 cargo : 108 tonnes
- Cruising speed : 990 km/h

Boeing 767- 300 ER 5 craft
- Length : 54.94 metres - Wingspan : 47.57 metres
- No. of seats : 206/210 - Cruising speed : 850 km/h

Boeing 737- 500/- 300/- 200 44 craft
- Length : 30.53/33.4 metres - Wingspan : 28.35/28.88 metres -
No. of seats : 112/134 - Cruising speed : 840 km/h

Concorde 5 craft
- Length : 62.13 metres - Wingspan : 25.56 metres
- No. of seats : 100 - Cruising speed 2,200 km/h

Airbus A340 - 300 19 craft
- Length : 59.42/63.69 metres - Wingspan : 60.30 metres
- No. of seats : 252 - Cruising speed : 860 km/h

Airbus A310-300/-200 10 craft
- Length : 46.66 metres - Wingspan : 43.9 metres
- No. of seats : 166/177 - Cruising speed : 860 km/h

Airbus A321 13 craft
- Length : 44.51 metres - Wingspan : 34.1 metres
- No. of seats : 188/206 - Cruising speed : 830 km/h

Airbus A319 20 craft
- Length : 30 metres - Wingspan : 34.1 metres
- No. of seats : 142 - Cruising speed 850 km/h

The increase in the number of craft in service

Air traffic is projected to increase at the rate of 5 per cent per year until 2015. The number of aircraft flying should grow from 2,000 to more than 3,000 in 2010. The range of large craft will expand the most, even though at the moment they only account for 20 per cent of planes against 75 per cent for medium-haul craft.

The A3XX/A380

A new Airbus, this is the plane of the future, with a capacity of 500 to 900 seats and a complete range of services offered to passengers: sleeping cabins, gym, shops ... Several dozen have already been ordered, 12 of which by Qantas, which is expecting delivery March 2006.

Travelling in good company

There are more than 300 airline companies operating in the world, but just a few of them attract the majority of passengers. They offer different services and a wide choice to travellers.

SCHEDULED AIRLINES
They fly their own planes on scheduled flights, of which the destinations and timetables are generally fixed twice a year (31 March and 31 October). These days they work in major partnerships with other airlines. One example is a London – Auckland flight, where passengers change from British Airways to Qantas planes at Perth.

Pluses : huge network, flexibility of timetables, more services, reliability.

Minuses : high fares, emphasis on 'business' destinations.

REGIONAL AIRLINES
These link up regional airports within the same country or across Europe. Their fares are high because their smaller planes cannot carry so many people and therefore do not make such a profit.

Pluses : improved access to less well-served cities, more services, reliability.

Minuses : fares often prohibitively expensive.

Obtaining information and buying tickets

The passenger can approach an airline company direct, but bearing in mind that 70 per cent of sales are made through travel agencies, which get preferential prices, a bargain is not necessarily guaranteed. However, airlines often offer promotions and discounted tickets, especially over the Internet. The benefit of a travel agency, though, is that it should have a good overview of the different airlines, routes and prices available.

Tour operators (or travel companies) charter planes or seats, or negotiate prices with scheduled airlines. Their services are sold in travel agencies, but they often have their own distribution networks. Companies have grown up which specialize in unsold seats: these are brokers or discount traders and often advertise on the Internet. If you buy from them at the last minute, you may get a good bargain, though you may have to search for it.

CHARTER AIRLINES

They fill their planes on behalf of a travel company (or on their own account if they have their own trading name) to a particular destination on a set date.

Pluses : lower fares; tourist destinations.

Minuses : 'unsociable' timetables, little flexibility, variable reliability, limited services.

LOW-COST AIRLINES

These companies, which first appeared in the United States, trim down their services in order to cut their costs and lower their fares. In Europe they mainly operate out of Britain, Ireland and the Benelux countries.

Pluses : ultra-competitive fares, regular services.

Minuses : limited network, minimum service, flying from minor airports, average reliability.

The great alliances

Airline companies have made agreements among themselves, allowing them to introduce joint loyalty schemes.

Earning air miles

Travellers can earn tickets by collecting air miles. Star Alliance (Lufthansa, United Airlines, Air Canada, British Midland, Singapore Airlines) One World (British Airways, American Airlines, Iberia, Qantas), Qualiflyer Group (Swissair, Sabena, TAP Air Portugal, AOM, Air Littoral), Wings (KLM. Alitalia, Continental Airlines) and Sky Team (Air France, Delta Airlines, Aeromexico, Korean Air) are the five big alliances. In principle, the more expensive your ticket, the more miles you earn. But air miles are also awarded for the distance travelled. A multiplier, varying with the tariff, is applied to the number of miles, but air miles are rarely, if ever, offered with discount tickets, and charter and low-cost companies do not qualify for air miles. Another way to earn air miles is by not flying at all. Some schemes offer air miles in return for goods or services such as petrol, dining and spending by credit card.

**SKYTEAM (Air France,
Delta Airlines, Aeromexico, Korean Air)**
Passengers carried : 174.3 million
Fleet : 685 craft
Daily flights (passengers and cargo) : 6,348
Destinations : 553
Members of loyalty scheme : 34.9 million
Staff : 151,000

The price of your ticket

The ticket price depends on many different things: a great many people on a plane may be paying a different price for the same journey. There are 76 different tariffs for the route between Paris and New York, with up to a fivefold difference between the cheapest and the most expensive.

Ticket prices: are they a rip-off?

A seat on an aeroplane is a perishable service: if it is empty on take-off it is no longer worth anything. Companies constantly have to juggle their fluctuating 'stocks' of seats, to achieve the maximum return. Passengers may occupy a similar 'class' of seat but may not have paid the same amount. For example, the ability to take the next plane instead of the one booked, to postpone a flight for 24 hours or even longer, often comes at a very high price. But this flexibility is what business passengers want and will pay for, and the airlines charge accordingly, explaining the high price of a so-called 'full-price' ticket, even in economy class. Conversely, the holder of a 'tourist-class' ticket, who can adhere to exact travel times will enjoy preferential rates.

PURCHASE/
HIRE OF CRAFT

15%

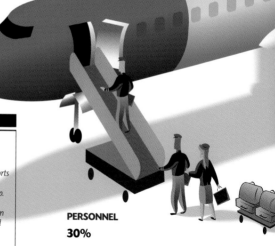

PERSONNEL

30%

AIRPORT TAXES: MORE EXPENSE

If you're flying with a major airline, airport taxes are invisible, included in the fare. On the other hand, tour operators generally advertise prices exclusive of airport taxes, in order to make the fare look more attractive. The difference can be considerable: in the United States taxes can exceed £30 for a return trip, or 10 per cent of the fare. Additionally, many airports levy taxes, payable in dollars, for the return trip. In reality, each airport operates its own tariff (on average between $15 and $30 (£10 to £20).

GENERAL EXPENSES, INSURANCE, GROUND-BASED SERVICES

13%

OPERATING PROFIT

5%

TAXES AND CHARGES

13%

FUEL

10%

These figures are averages, reflecting the structure of the costs of the major scheduled airline companies. They can vary considerably, depending on the airline, the types of craft and the level of service provided.

COMMERCIAL EXPENSES AND MARKETING

8%

SERVICING AND MAINTENANCE OF PLANES

6%

SOURCES : COMUTA, 1ST QUARTER 2000

A TICKET IN TWO PARTS

The two parts are detachable on boarding. The one on the right is for the passenger; keep it in case you need to claim *afterwards: for air miles, delays, flight cancellations ... The flight coupon, on the left, is for the airline.*

City and airport (and terminal where applicable) of departure

Date of issue of ticket

Class of reservation. Originally there were three classes (F for first, C for business and Y for economy). Today there aren't enough letters in the alphabet to provide a code for all the different fares.

Operator's international code (each company has its own code: BM for British Midland, LH for Lufthansa, CX for Cathay Pacific, DL for Delta Airlines) and flight number

Conditions for refund on ticket

Ticket price

Airport taxes and passenger charges

Amount payable, inclusive of taxes

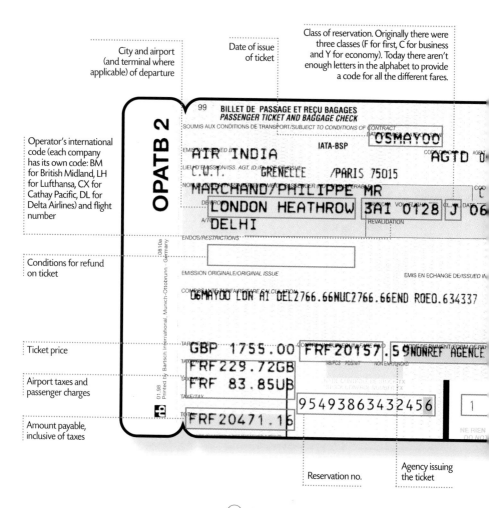

99 BILLET DE PASSAGE ET REÇU BAGAGES
PASSENGER TICKET AND BAGGAGE CHECK
SOUMIS AUX CONDITIONS DE TRANSPORT/SUBJECT TO CONDITIONS OF CONTRACT

OPATB 2

IATA-BSP

O5MAYOO

AIR INDIA AGTD O

C.W.T. GRENELLE /PARIS 75015

MARCHAND/PHILIPPE MR

LONDON HEATHROW 3AI 0128 J 06

DELHI

O6MAYOO LON AI DEL2766.66NUC2766.66END ROEO.634337

GBP 1755.00 FRF20157.59NONREF AGENCE

FRF 229.72GB

FRF 83.85UB

FRF20471.16

9549386343 2456

1

Reservation no.

Agency issuing the ticket

What does your ticket say ?

An ATB (automatic boarding) travel ticket is non-transferable: it is an authorisation to travel and serves as a contract between the airline and the passenger. It is also proof of payment.

Reservation status:
OK for firm booking,
LL for waiting list,
OPEN for an open ticket

Date by which the ticket should be used

Name of passenger

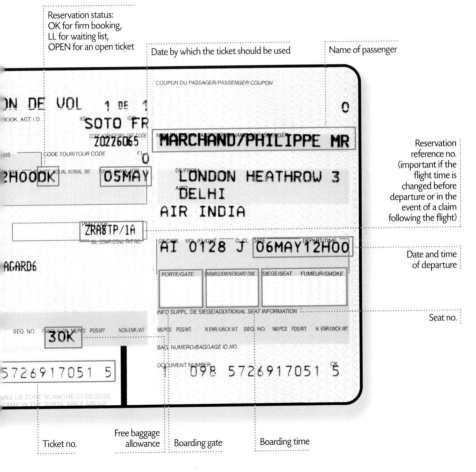

Reservation reference no. (important if the flight time is changed before departure or in the event of a claim following the flight)

Date and time of departure

Seat no.

Ticket no.

Free baggage allowance

Boarding gate

Boarding time

COUPON DU PASSAGER/PASSENGER COUPON

)N DE VOL   1 DE 1   0

3OOK. AGT. I.D.   IIS   'SOTO FR   ISO
                        Z0276065   MARCHAND/PHILIPPE MR
3IS   CODE TOUR/TOUR CODE   FI   0
2HOOOK   05MAY   DE/FROM 'LONDON HEATHROW 3
                              A/TO 'DELHI
                              AIR INDIA
        PART FARE
        ZRR8TP/1A
        BIL. COMP./CONJ. TKT. NO.   AI 0128 J 06MAY12H00

AGARD6   PORTE/GATE   EMBARQUEMENT/BOARD TIME   SIEGE/SEAT   FUMEUR/SMOKE

                                      INFO SUPPL. DE SIEGE/ADDITIONAL SEAT INFORMATION
SEQ. NO.   PDS/WT.   NON ENR./WT.   NB/PCS PDS/WT.   N ENR./UNCK.WT.   SEQ. NO.   NB/PCS PDS/WT.   N. ENR/UNCK.WT.
        30K
                                      BAG. NUMERO/BAGGAGE ID NO.
5726917051 5   DOCUMENT NUMBER 1   098 5726917051 5
ANS LA ZONE BLANCHE CI-DESSUS
TAMP IN THE WHITE AREA ABOVE

A town in miniature

Large modern airports are hives of activity, with restaurants, post offices, chapels, cinemas and row upon row of shops.

The works!
Travellers who have to spend time in these vast complexes of glass and steel are more and more demanding in terms of the services they require, which is why Singapore airport has opened a swimming pool, and London Heathrow has a beauty salon, so you can freshen up after a long flight.

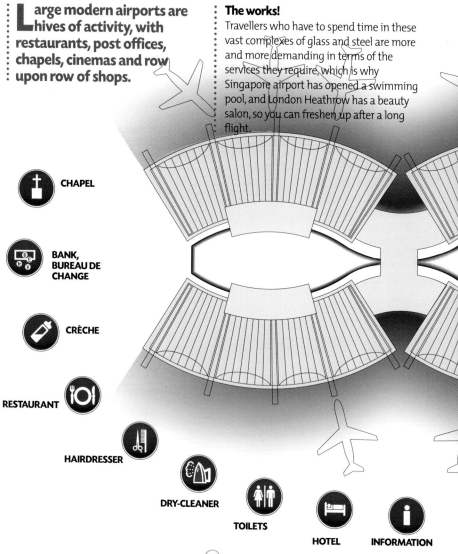

CHAPEL

BANK, BUREAU DE CHANGE

CRÈCHE

RESTAURANT

HAIRDRESSER

DRY-CLEANER

TOILETS

HOTEL

INFORMATION

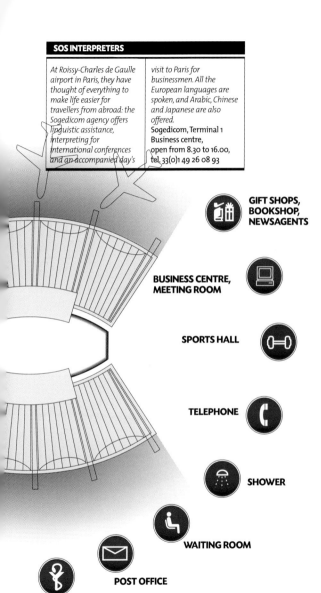

SOS INTERPRETERS

At Roissy-Charles de Gaulle airport in Paris, they have thought of everything to make life easier for travellers from abroad: the Sogedicom agency offers linguistic assistance, interpreting for international conferences and an accompanied day's	visit to Paris for businessmen. All the European languages are spoken, and Arabic, Chinese and Japanese are also offered. Sogedicom, Terminal 1 Business centre, open from 8.30 to 16.00, tel. 33(0)1 49 26 08 93

GIFT SHOPS, BOOKSHOP, NEWSAGENTS

BUSINESS CENTRE, MEETING ROOM

SPORTS HALL

TELEPHONE

SHOWER

WAITING ROOM

POST OFFICE

PHARMACY, FIRST AID

AMSTERDAM-SCHIPHOL: AT THE FOREFRONT OF INNOVATION

Schiphol is the only airport in the world that lies below sea level. It is also one of the most important airports for international flights in the Netherlands, which has no internal flights. In 1999 410,000 planes and 37.11 million passengers passed through. It is the fourth biggest airport in Europe after Heathrow (62.2 million), Frankfurt (45.8 million) and Roissy-Charles de Gaulle (43.6 million), and it is the eleventh biggest in the world. Within Europe it is one of the most innovative and best equipped. Numerous services are provided – a crèche to look after baby while you go shopping; a sauna and showers, very popular with travellers who have sometimes spent many hours on a plane; a sports hall and fitness suite; a casino; a dry cleaner; a business centre with offices that can be booked (with fax, telephones and computers available) in addition to a service for hiring telephones and computers; and a meeting room for multinational companies, which bring their managers together here from all over Europe.

Transport into town

Your first contact with a new country comes on leaving the airport. Try to research the different methods of transport available from the airport before your departure and remember to have some cash in the appropriate currency with you.

Some basic rules

A fairly basic, but useful rule is to avoid taxis in rush hours. If you do take one, try to find out in advance roughly what the fare should be. Some airports, such as Miami, operate a system of pre-payment to avoid any problem, while at others a fixed rate may be stipulated, such as the ride into Manhattan from JFK airport. If you are watching your budget and have the time, a bus or coach is usually a good option. Finally, the train or metro, where such a link exists, is usually a very efficient way of getting into a city. However, you may find that the train or metro station is not near the airport building itself and that you need to take a shuttle bus to reach it.

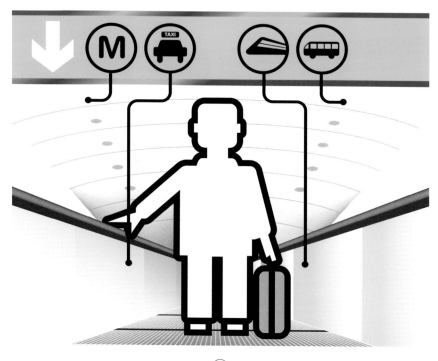

Security checks

Complying with the rules and checks on passengers and luggage are the inevitable prelude to any plane trip.

X-ray checks

Luggage is checked after registration. The contents show up on the screen of an X-ray machine. These are usually described as 'film-safe' for undeveloped camera film, but if you have fast film (1000ASA/31 DIN or over) it will be safer to hand it over separately.

Metal detectors

Passengers pass under these archways and any metal objects are detected. Their sensitivity varies from one country to another: in the United States, for example, some can even detect the metallic packaging around a packet of cigarettes.

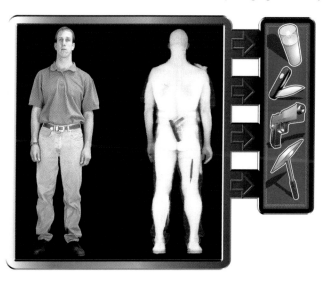

NOT ALLOWED IN CABIN

Apart from firearms, you might be surprised by the list of objects that are not allowed in the cabin. A toy that looks like a weapon, or any 'object which could induce fear', will not be allowed. This is also the case with Swiss army penknives with a blade longer than 8 cm (5 in). Leave aerosols (perfume, toiletries, medicines) holding more than 500 ml (13$^1/_2$ fl. oz), ice-picks, harpoons and self-defence sprays in the hold as well. There are many restrictions on hold baggage too: no aerosols over 2 litres nor any camping gas cylinders, for instance.

CAREFUL WITH A PACEMAKER!

If you have a heart pacemaker, you should tell the security guard and you should not go through the metal detectors. Your security check will be done manually. The same precaution should be taken by people wearing hearing aids.

Unattended luggage

Any luggage abandoned or even simply left unattended for a few minutes runs the risk of being destroyed by security staff, without warning, and certainly without any compensation for the owner.

The movement of passengers and their goods

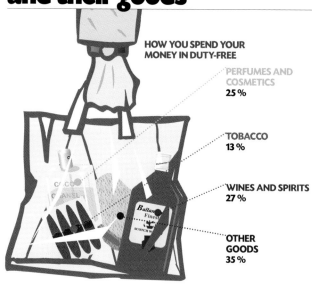

HOW YOU SPEND YOUR MONEY IN DUTY-FREE

PERFUMES AND COSMETICS
25 %

TOBACCO
13 %

WINES AND SPIRITS
27 %

OTHER GOODS
35 %

Since duty-free shopping is only for passengers travelling out of the European Union, your boarding card will be requested at the tills to check your destination.

Goodbye to duty free in Europe

Since midnight 30 June 1999 duty free has not been allowed between EU countries, a trade estimated to be worth £4.5 billion in Europe. The BAA airports in the UK alone estimate a loss of £35 million in profits from its demise, but economists disagree over the financial effects on passengers. See page 81 for information on your duty-free allowance travelling outside Europe.

DUTY-FREES WITH A LOCAL FLAVOUR

1 - Amsterdam
Tulips in all shapes and colours, cut flowers or bulbs.

2 - Copenhagen
Whole or sliced smoked salmon, fish pâté, cod roe ... northern flavours to tickle your taste buds.

3 - Dubai
Never pass through this airport without a lucky horseshoe (and a credit card): stupendous raffles are regularly run here. A ticket costs £90, but the prizes are attractive: you could win a Porsche or a Ferrari.

4 - Dublin
Real Guinness flows freely, and a wide range of products is available bearing the famous logo. Take it steady though: you don't want to miss your flight ...

5 - Frankfurt
Whips, suspender belts and other titillating stuff ... your mind is sure to wander in the only sex shop found in an airport.

The European Shengen area

Since 1994 the Shengen agreement has provided for the free movement of people among the ten European countries that signed it. Consequently there is no longer any systematic checking within airports of passengers travelling between the ten countries. However, a valid identity card or passport remains necessary for travel throughout the EU; it will be requested on registration by the carrier, which will have the right to refuse embarkation to any passenger who does not have the appropriate documents in his or her possession.

Customs in the European Union

It is possible to buy and transport any number of goods within the European Union. Some exceptions are arms and ammunition, objects of cultural value, some types of protected species of flora and fauna and derivative products, live animals and medicines.

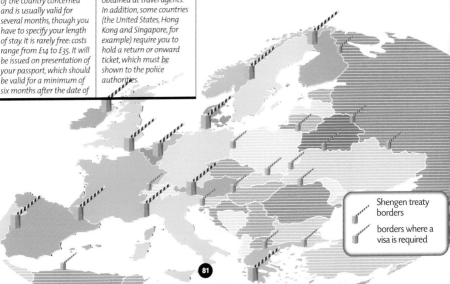

Shengen treaty borders

borders where a visa is required

WHAT YOU NEED TO KNOW

DO YOU REALLY NEED TO BE AT THE AIRPORT TWO HOURS BEFORE DEPARTURE ?

The latest official times for registration vary from airport to airport and depend on type of flight (international, European or domestic). It also depends on the airline. At London Heathrow's Terminal 3, for instance, Qantas require 2 hours and Gulf Air 1½. Aer Lingus, at Terminal 1, only requires 20 minutes.

Airlines try to stagger the check-in procedure for flights by getting tourists to register as early as possible, leaving business passengers free to register as late as possible. A minimum time would be 20 minutes for domestic, 30 for European and 45 for international flights. However, be aware that you will probably lose any pre-reserved seats if you check in this late.

OVERBOOKING

Passengers' seats are not guaranteed: airlines know from experience that some people with reservations will not check in – this happens with nearly every flight and can account for as many as 30 per cent of reservations. They therefore have to allow for this and frequently overbook flights. You have to arrive early to be among the first on the stand-by waiting list, but you will be among the last to board. If it should happen that there is no seat for your reservation, the airlines are obliged to pay compensation to any passenger with a confirmed reservation. (See also page 116.) To try to avoid this, arrive well within the check-in time.

Immediate embarkation

For regular travellers, taking the plane is a well-developed ritual, while for those who fly only occasionally, a trip can require real organisation and planning. There are some things that everyone needs to remember for a stress-free departure.

CHANGING PLANES - IN TRANSIT

On a trip that involves several stops and several airlines, the first carrier registers the passenger for the whole journey and gives him or her all the boarding cards for the flights. The passenger will usually receive his luggage at the final destination, without having to worry about the changes of plane. Known as 'inter-lining' baggage, this is possible only between airline companies that have made commercial agreements. Airline companies are trying to cut the waiting times between changes of flight. These are currently at least 20 to 40 minutes for Europe and 45 to 60 minutes for intercontinental flights.

TIMETABLE FOR BOARDING

Minus 50 minutes: Dozens of things have to be done before the passengers board. The APU, a small turbine situated in the tail of the plane, is started to provide an electrical supply and air-conditioning in the cabin.

Minus 30 minutes: The first passengers board. The plane fills up, starting with the rear seats. The cabin staff see that this all runs smoothly.

Minus 5 minutes: The captain is given the final load distribution manifest (trim and mass) to check and sign.

Take-off time: The doors are closed. Clearance to start the engines and reverse the plane is requested from the control tower. Fasten your safety belts.

In the capable hands of the crew

Pilots, ground staff, technical crew and their assistants all work together, preparing the flight down to the smallest detail. An aircraft is in service for between 900 and 1,200 hours a year, including preparation times in airports.

Flight preparation

This begins 2½ hours before the time at which the plane is due to leave its parking place.

Departure minus 2½ hours : The crew arrives at the assembly point, called 'check-in' or 'departure'. A flight report is given to the pilots, who check through several points: the weather forecast for the country of departure, the country of destination and countries to which the flight might be diverted; technical details for the flight; routes, temperatures and wind speeds; information on airports on the route; staff on strike, runways closed; the numbers of passengers flying in each class; special travellers, children, disabled people, VIPs; and the nature of the cargo. All this affects the amount of fuel required.

Departure minus 1 hour : The crew comes on board. The organisation of the plane is shared among the hostesses, the stewards and the pilots. The pilots adjust the instruments and load the computers. The tanks are filled with fuel, and the passengers come on board. Finally, the captain signs the docket for 'load (freight + passengers + fuel) and trim (distribution of the load)'.

Departure : The plane takes off.

The cabin crew

Training courses generally last from 10 to 12 weeks. The job calls for patience and efficiency, and includes soothing nervous passengers, looking after their children, dealing with health problems, as well as serving meals – sometimes at some speed – keeping accounts and managing the stocks of goods sold on board. Success depends on keeping calm when faced with a variety of challenging situations. The crew has regular drills to practise the evacuation of passengers in the shortest possible time. They have special life-saving certificates and should know, among other things, how to deliver a baby in flight! Their job is physically demanding: they walk about 20 km (12½ miles) in the course of a transatlantic flight. In the non-PC 1960s a hostess would only stay in the job for an average of 18 months because the age limit was 30 and single status was obligatory.

AFDS: Autopilot flight-director system: allows selection of routes, cruising speed, ascent and descent, cruising Mach and angle of descent.

Gyroscopic artificial horizon: electromechanical instrument.

Lever for lowering and raising the landing gear.

Attitude Display Indicator (ADI): monitoring the position of the plane, ie its pitch, and its speed.

Horizontal Situation Indicator screen showing route and weather radar returns (HSI).

Vertical and horizontal flight management system (FMS), allowing the route to be verified after having entered the route markers (waypoints).

Electronic display (ECAM) which includes central warning gauges to check on the functioning of the engines and the various systems (pressurisation, electrical circuits, hydraulics and so on).

THE CAPTAIN AND CO-PILOT

After getting his licence, a pilot has to take regular tests on a simulator as well as undergo medical examinations. A captain is always a former co-pilot, and promotion depends primarily on seniority. His salary is partly linked to the size of aircraft he flies. The captain has complete authority on the aircraft. He can order anyone causing a problem to be restrained until landing.

Where should you sit on the plane?

For a typical London–New York journey, passengers could have paid 76 different prices for their seats. You could say that no two people have paid the same . With a fivefold difference in price between the cheapest and most expensive, is this a rip-off?

Smoking or non-smoking?

Domestic and European flights are now non-smoking only. Transatlantic flights are increasingly becoming so. In fact, it is only on some flights to Asia and Africa that nicotine addicts do not have to bite their nails.

Window or aisle seat?

Some airlines will reserve a seat when you book, but to stand a chance of obtaining the seat you want, arrive well within the check-in time. It is not an easy choice on a long-haul flight. Opt for the window to have a quiet sleep or admire the view, unless you're level with the wings, of course. With an aisle seat, you won't disturb others if you want to get out, but you will in turn be disturbed by others. In order not to feel hemmed in, avoid the middle seats in a 2-3-2 or 3-5-3 configuration.

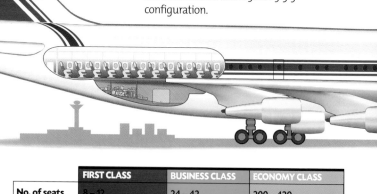

	FIRST CLASS	BUSINESS CLASS	ECONOMY CLASS
No. of seats	8 – 12	24 – 42	200 – 420
Angle seat reclines	140º – 180º	115º – 150º	90º – 96º
Space between rows	160 – 200 cm (5 – 6 ft)	120 – 145 cm (4 ft – 4 ft 9 in)	76 – 92 cm (2 ft 6 in – 3 ft)

Front or back?

Taller people

Six-footers will be best off in the first row of seats in front of the emergency exits, which have more leg room. Again, arriving early will increase the chances of obtaining one of these seats.

Disturbance

There is less noise at the front of the plane, but turbulence is felt the least in seats level with the wings. Generally speaking, the further you are from the centre of gravity of the plane, the more you are affected by turbulence, so seats at the rear or front of the cabin will be more affected than those that are level with the wings.

Looking after a baby?

You have priority on the first row of each zone as there is enough space here to put a cot on the floor and often a fold-down table on the bulkhead to secure it and improve accessibility in flight. Some airlines, British Airways for example, will usually pre-board families with babies before the main rush begins.

Smokers

The last rows in each class are generally reserved for smokers when smoking is permitted on board. Note that you might not be able to recline your seat in the very last of these rows.

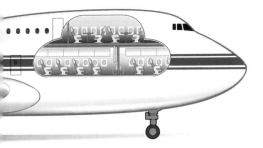

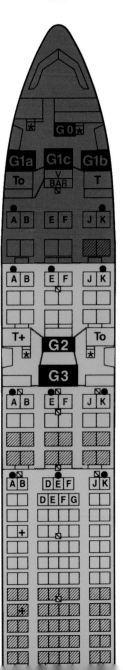

FIRST CLASS

BUSINESS CLASS

ECONOMY CLASS

Special categories of traveller

Special rules and conditions apply
for children, pregnant women and
disabled travellers. British Airways rules
are used here as an example, but most
airlines have broadly similar rules.

Children from 0 to 2 years

In a plane children are technically infants
until the age of two. They may travel free of
charge on domestic flights and for only 10
per cent of the fare on international flights
if travelling on their parent's knee. Up to
two years old, infant seats, fitting on the
bulkhead, can be provided free of charge,
but are limited in number – a maximum
of 12 on a 747, for instance. For children from
6 months to 36 months old, parents may
provide their own car seat for the infant to
sit in, but this will be strapped into a seat
and will be subject to the child fare –
between 50 and 67 per cent of the normal
fare. A limited number of special carry-cots
are available for children under six months

old (ask about this when you make your
reservation). Only on US routes is a baggage
allowance made for children under 2 – one
bag only.

Children from 2 to 12 years

They are required to travel in a seat, but see

above for car seat use. They are subject to the child fare.

Children from 12 to 18 years

The child must pay full fare. Scheduled airlines accept unaccompanied adolescents from the age of 12 years; they will make efforts to help should the need arise but do not take legal responsibility. On charters, some travel companies will only take them unaccompanied from the age of 16.

Unaccompanied children

The tariffs are the same as for the previous age group. The child may travel alone from 6 to 12 years old after completing a 'Young Flyer Declaration'; any younger and special clearance is needed. The UM (unaccompanied minor) procedure is lengthy; allow at least ten days to arrange it. The airline will only accept responsibility between the airports of departure and arrival and UMs cannot be accepted as stand-by passengers.

DISABLED PEOPLE: STILL A WAY TO GO

Whatever the disability, it is strongly recommended that you contact the airline before your trip. Many airports throughout the world - and all airports in Europe - have facilities for physically disabled people, and airline companies have improved conditions for them. But it is still difficult for them to board planes. It is, for example, still impossible to move around a plane in a wheelchair. There was a notorious incident in 1999 when Air France refused to carry an overweight passenger on the grounds that he took up the space of two seats and should therefore pay for two tickets.

THE DOG (AND THE CAT) COMES TOO!

The rules vary according to airline. Some allow animals under 5 kg (11 lb) to travel with their owner in the cabin, in a bag or a cage, though others companies will allow this only in exceptional circumstances, so you should check before you travel. British Airways, for instance, do not allow any pets in the cabin. Animals weighing over 5 kg (11 lb) must travel in the hold, which is heated and pressurised, in a specially designed cage sold by the airlines (generally costing between £42 to £133 depending on the size of the animal). On international flights the charge is often at the same rate as for excess baggage: it will cost about 1.5 per cent of the economy class ticket price per kilogram (2.2 lb) of animal. But an animal is not counted as part of your luggage allowance, and you will still have to pay even if you are travelling without other luggage or if your luggage weighs less than the allowance. Only guide dogs are allowed in the cabin free of charge, and then only by some companies. Do not forget your best friend's vaccination certificate or its health declaration. Before you travel, contact the airline to find out what documents you will need to supply. Finally, some countries do not allow any domestic animals at all across their borders: check with the embassy or airline.

Managing your luggage

Knowing how to pack your cases and hand luggage, and what to put in each, will smooth your journey and will make things much simpler should anything go astray. Remember that you will be charged for excess baggage.

IN THE CABIN

The airline company has the right to put into the hold any hand luggage it considers too large or too heavy, with the maximum combined weight allowed on British Airways, for example, being 18 kg (40 lb) for first and business (2 bags permitted), and 6 kg (13 lb) for economy (1 piece only).

Never put in the hold ...

Valuable items: in case of theft, the carrier's responsibility is fairly limited.

Medicines: if you are going to need to take them when you arrive, don't forget that luggage can get held up ... or even lost.

House keys : because they might get lost.

Fragile items : luggage in the hold is never handled with care.

IN THE HOLD

Your ticket generally gives you a free allowance of at least 20 kg (44 lb), but this varies according to airline, route and class. For example, the allowance on British Airways to most of the world is 23 kg (51 lb) in World, World Plus and Euro Traveller, 30 kg (66 lb) in Club World and Club Europe and 40 kg (88 lb) in First. If this is exceeded, the passenger has to pay a surcharge, British Airways charging from £3.54 per kilo (London–Rome) to £16 per kilo (London–Australia). Don't forget to lock your luggage.

Should you put your home address on the outside label of your luggage? Think carefully before you do so because teams of crooks or dishonest employees have been known to pick out the addresses of holidaymakers and pass them on to burglars who pay a visit to the occupants' homes while they are away. The answer? Put your business address on the label or use a concealed label.

ONE PIECE OF LUGGAGE ALLOWED ON BOARD

Combined dimensions (length + width + height) usually cannot exceed 115 cm (45 in) – for example, a suitcase of 40 x 55 x 20 cm (15 x 22 x 8 in). This figure can be greater on some airlines.

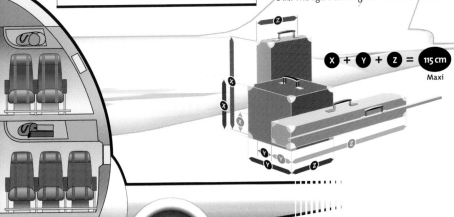

$$X + Y + Z = 115\ cm$$

Maxi

LARGE OBJECTS AND BULKY FREIGHT

Some bulky objects (windsurfers, large domestic appliances) can only travel as freight. To be sure that they travel on the same flight as you, you need to inform the airline in advance and arrive at least three hours before departure. The average charge for this type of transport is between 70p and £3.50 per kilo (2.2 lb) depending on the destination (but usually there is free allowance worth around £21). Cars and motorbikes can also travel on the same flight as you but the number of cars allowed on each flight is restricted, and prices vary greatly depending on destination, company and vehicle.

SOS LOST LUGGAGE

At the airport each item is given a ticket by the airline, and the passenger is given a receipt, usually in the form of a sticker attached to the ticket stub. These little pieces of paper hold the information for all the flights your suitcase will travel on. Officially, two pieces of luggage go astray per 1,000. That is the equivalent of one lost piece of luggage per Boeing 747! A piece of luggage is usually considered lost if it isn't found within 21 days. They do usually turn up within 24 hours. (See page 117 for further information.)

Relax, the aeroplane is the safest means of transport in the world

Lloyds, the London insurer, says that air travel is 25 times safer than a car journey. In spite of this, many of us fear bad weather, are sensitive to the movements of the craft and listen out for strange noises. Here are some facts that you may find useful, either to put your own mind at rest or to reassure your companion or neighbour.

Before take-off

A slight whistling signals that the jet engines are starting up. Loud bumps are the luggage holds being closed underneath your feet. Then the plane taxies to the end of the runway where it gets into position and opens up its engines at full throttle, while remaining still. After a few seconds, the pilot releases the brakes and the plane shoots forward. The plane is built to fly, and on the ground it is no more than a clumsy bus with landing gear that responds noisily to any bumps in the runway.

Cruising

The plane takes off quickly, and a succession of possibly quite loud noises indicates that the landing gear has been retracted (under the wings and at the front of the plane) and the hatches closed. These same noises will be repeated when the plane is about to land. Repetitive hissing sounds shortly after take-off mean that the flaps, which extend the wing to increase lift, are retracting. These same flaps are used on landing as youill see if you have a window seat. Although this may be a cause for concern for nervous flyers, the process actually makes take-off and landing safer.

Getting back to earth

Landing is seldom very rough, but it is often followed by a very marked increase in the noise levels from the jet engines, which are thrown into reverse to slow the plane down.

THE CHANGE IN SHAPE OF A PLANE WING THAT OCCURS WHEN THE AEROFOIL FLAPS AND THE AIRBRAKES ARE IN USE

Don't necessarily alter your plans for your trip on account of a bad weather forecast: the conditions on the ground are not the same as those you will meet at high altitude.

Strong winds

This is an advantage for take-off and landing, which are always performed into the wind. The stronger the wind, the faster take-off and landing can happen. If you fly often into the same airport, you will not always see the same view as you come in to land; this is because the plane may approach the runway from either end, depending where the prevailing wind is coming from.

Storms

A plane's fuselage shields the inside from electricity in the form of electromagnetic energy, which means it is completely protected from lightning, though flashes of lightning can be impressive seen through the window.

Fog

Nearly all airports and planes are equipped today for landing and take-off in conditions of reduced visibility, although it still sometimes happens that planes are diverted to another airport. All craft have reserves of fuel that will allow them to divert if they need to.

Snow and ice

Planes have systems for de-icing on the wing. But wings may be weighed down by ice when the plane is on the ground. Before take-off in these conditions, the plane is sprayed with an anti-freeze mixture of alcohol and water.

Turbulence

The crew can often tell from weather radar where patches of turbulence are and ask you to fasten your seat belts. Turbulence may not be pleasant, but it doesn't threaten the safety of the aircraft. However, it can throw people around the cabin, so do fasten your belts!

YOUR SKIN AND EYES: MOISTURISE ON LONG FLIGHTS

In the cabin the air is dry: it has no more than 10 per cent humidity. Regular moisturising is therefore recommended, particularly on long flights. Drink at least 1 litre (1¾ pt) of water every four to five hours. If your skin is very sensitive, take a water spray and use a moisturising cream before the flight and when you arrive. During the flight, wear glasses rather than contact lenses as the lack of humidity will also dry your eyes. If you are prone to dry eyes take some eye drops along too. Also take your sunglasses, as the reflection from the clouds can tire your eyes and the sun can be strong if it is on your side of the aircraft.

YOUR EARS: UNDER PRESSURE IN FLIGHT

On take-off and especially on landing, atmospheric pressure changes greatly, causing problems, particularly blocked ears and buzzing sounds. In extreme cases an ear drum can even rupture. At these times in the flight, the following might help: unblock your ears (to salivate more chew gum or suck a citrus sweet), yawn (by opening your mouth wide you take the pressure off your eardrums), blow out with your mouth closed, holding your nose (as if you were trying to force air out through your ears). All this helps to re-establish pressure in various parts of the eardrum. A baby can be given his bottle or a dummy.

FOR YOUR COMFORT IN THE CABIN

• A pair of light tennis shoes, preferably made of cotton, or slippers • Loose, comfortable clothing • A warm pullover or shawl . • A lightweight scarf, or silk or cotton headsquare • A blindfold and earplugs • Eye drops	• A mineral water spray • Moisturising cream • A U-shaped inflatable neck cushion • Citrus sweets or chewing gum • Nicotine patch or gum for smokers (on non-smoking flights)	• A light herbal sedative to help you sleep • For your arrival, a wash bag (with deodorant and toothbrush) • A bottle of mineral water, although the cabin crew should bring you a glass of water on request.

Feeling good in flight

So-called 'economy class sickness' is now of real concern, especially to those who travel long haul. Sitting still for long periods in a confined space can lead to embolism for those at risk. However, the World Health Organisation reports that the transmission of infectious disease is lower on board an aircraft than in a bus or train.

GUARD AGAINST SORE THROATS

A plane cruises at around 10,000 metres (33,000 ft) and the external temperature is around -50°C (122°F). Thanks to the pressurisation the atmospheric pressure inside is close to that found at 2,000 metres (6,600 ft). As a result of this pressurisation and the air-conditioning on board, a plane can feel cool. Blankets are usually provided, but it is a good idea to have a scarf, shawl or pullover handy. Your body will also feel cooler as it is sedentary for long periods and it is not always feasible to warm up by moving about

LEG ROOM

The distance between your seat and the seat in front (known as seat pitch) varies according to the aircraft. Seats in standard economy class generally have less leg room, usually close to the legal minimum of 66 cm (26 in), than the 'enhanced' economy offered by Virgin Atlantic, British Airways and British Midland with 96 cm (38 in), for example. Business and first classes	*offer even more. This is a factor that plays a part in 'economy class sickness' as the more restricted the seating space, the less you can move about. Extra leg room comes at a price, however. The cheapest round-trip fare to New York is about £200; for premium economy just over £1,000; and for business class about £3,500.*

SEAT PITCH

A useful web site listing seat pitches can be found at www.aviation-health.org

SWOLLEN LEGS AND ANKLES

Your blood circulation will slow down under the effect of reduced pressure. The common symptoms are swelling of the feet and ankles, feelings of heaviness and pins and needles in the legs. To reduce the risk of embolism and phlebitis, and particularly if you are prone to circulation problems, it is very important that you don't sit still for the whole flight. Move around the cabin regularly if possible. If this is difficult, make sure that you exercise regularly in your seat. Recommended exercises include; raising your thighs, lifting your feet off the floor and rotating them from side to side. Take off heavy or close-fitting shoes and wear slippers or light shoes and wear loose comfortable clothing. If you know or suspect you have circulation problems, consult a doctor before flying.

New technology on board

Seat-back screens for watching films to playing roulette: passengers now have at their disposal the latest technological innovations to combat boredom and reduce their stress.

Beware of interference

Electronic equipment emits rays that can cause interference with the navigation systems. The use of personal computers and CD players is prohibited during take-off and landing. The use of mobile phones is prohibited at any time during the flight. Anyone who flouts these regulations may have their equipment confiscated by the captain and may face a fine.

TELEPHONE
Some airlines have installed phones, sometimes in individual seats, but on board a plane a phone call has to be transmitted by satellite, and this can be very expensive: £3.50 for connection and from £2 to £7 per minute for the call. Remember that you are not allowed to use your mobile phone on board, or have it switched on, as it can dangerously interfere with aircraft systems.

INDIVIDUAL SCREEN
You no longer have to put up with your film being spoilt by the head of the passenger in the row in front. Airlines are installing individual screens in the backs of the seats of the row in front. The size of screen varies depending on the class you are in: the prize currently goes to Singapore Airlines with a 36 cm (14 in) screen in first class.

HIDDEN CAMERAS

A camera fixed to the front of certain aircraft films the whole flight. This is intended as a measure to reduce the anxiety felt by those passengers who find taking off and landing particularly nerve-racking. They can follow the whole process on a small screen.

A CHOICE OF CHANNELS

Passengers with individual screens usually have the choice of several channels, offering a varied choice of programmes: films, documentaries, cartoons ... It's not that easy to draw up a viewing schedule. Films have to appeal to majority tastes, then they may have to be subtitled into different languages and censored to take out anything which could shock: violent scenes, nudity and, obviously, air disasters!

NOISE-COMPENSATING HEADPHONES

A real boon for music lovers, these headphones reflect away the noise of the plane, leaving a much clearer music track.

PLAYING HARD

It is now possible to gamble on some planes. Games such as roulette or black jack are now available on new entertainment systems (via personal screens). Bets are paid for by banker's card. But a 'flying casino' is difficult to run: apart from the various forms of legislation applicable in different countries, authorities are also worried about the potentially impulsive reactions of the players. British Airways has set a limit on losses of £70 in economy class, £250 in business class and £350 in first class.

Those hooked on computer games can also indulge their habit on board now, with no threat to their bank balances. Video games are diverting and help some passengers control their stress levels and aggressive instincts.

TWO CHEERS FOR THE IN-FLIGHT OFFICE

Business travellers are not too keen on working in-flight, judging by their response to the services offered to them. Fax machines and telephones are used very little. The airlines that introduced office services on board have been doing some rethinking, and the planned installation of connections for computers is not really causing much excitement either. Relaxing, reading and resting seem to be much more popular mid-air activities.

Booking via the Net

The increase in air traffic forecast for the next few years will no doubt be augmented by the continued development of electronic communications. For the airlines, it means savings on their overheads and the chance to build up the loyalty of their passengers by offering them various advantages.

Taking off with the Net

On the Internet you can reserve and buy tickets on-line, check timetables and whether flights are disrupted, find out information about other services offered by the airline, plan your arrival at your destination airport so that you can move on as quickly as possible and find out a little about the nearby tourist attractions. Travel is big on the Internet, and holidays and flights are one of the four products most often sold on-line, along with computer products, books and music. Sales of flights on the Internet are projected to be worth £8.4 billion in 2002 (Source: Jupiter Bureau).

SECURE PAYMENTS ON THE INTERNET

As with payments with a banker's card, there is a security risk when paying over the Internet. But people have tended to worry more about paying via the Internet as everything seems so open. In response to this, encryption software, which scrambles the card number, has been installed by most companies, making Internet payments safer now than telephone payments. In addition, most banks cover the risk associated with using a banker's card – an indication of how small they think the risk is.

Mutually beneficial

Airlines and airport services also experience less pressure at their desks and on their phone lines as a result of Internet bookings. The *Frequently asked questions* (FAQ) list is useful for giving out information: some sites post these lists of FAQs in which the most common questions are answered, saving time and money for both passenger and airline.

Beating jet lag

Jet lag, caused by travelling between time zones, is becoming a common ailment for frequent travellers: for 94 per cent it is a nuisance and for 45 per cent it is a real problem. It is caused by disruption to the internal biological clock.

Better west than east

Your biological clock is disturbed if you just move into the next time zone , but jet lag becomes a problem once you have passed through three or four time zones, and is also dependent on your direction of travel. If you go north or south, you won't notice any difference. If you travel west you will be in advance of yourself as far as your internal clock is concerned. A trip from Paris to New York causes fewer problems than a New York–London trip, because west-to-east journeys make you late compared to your internal clock. Digestive problems, tiredness and sleep disruption are the main problems. It's estimated that the body takes one day to get over each hour of time difference.

Adjust your routine

For a short trip (three days maximum) try to keep to the pattern of the country you have left. In the case of a trip of more than a week, adjust as quickly as possible to the time of the country in which you are staying.

The biological clock

Light, whether sunlight or ultraviolet light, can fool the biological clock. When you are travelling west, 'take in' the light until as late as possible; when you travel east, avoid daylight if you can from the middle of the afternoon onwards in order to simulate darkness and to encourage the onset of sleep as early as possible.

Do not tire yourself before a journey

Jet lag puts your body under a lot of strain – don't give it even more to cope with. Put bluntly, don't overdo it the night before your flight.

Fly healthily

Get as much sleep as possible on the plane, relax your body and do not take stimulants, such as tobacco, alcohol or coffee, but do drink plenty of water.

MELATONIN - A SECRET WEAPON?

Melatonin is a hormone that is secreted during the night by the pituitary gland. It is now believed that it contributes to the quality of sleep, which has led to the idea of taking it as a supplement when biological rhythms have been disrupted. In the United States melatonin is classed as a dietary supplement rather than as a drug. It is therefore sold freely, and there are no strict controls over its manufacture. The dose recommended by airline staff associations is between 3 mg and 10 mg, to be taken on arrival and one hour before going to bed, until the jet lag has passed. In Europe, the sale of melatonin is often prohibited, as in Britain and France, as ultimately the long-term side-effects have not been proved.

WHEN IT'S MIDNIGHT IN TOKYO IT'S 3PM IN LONDON,
WHEN IT'S 3 PM IN LONDON, IT'S 10 AM IN NEW YORK ...

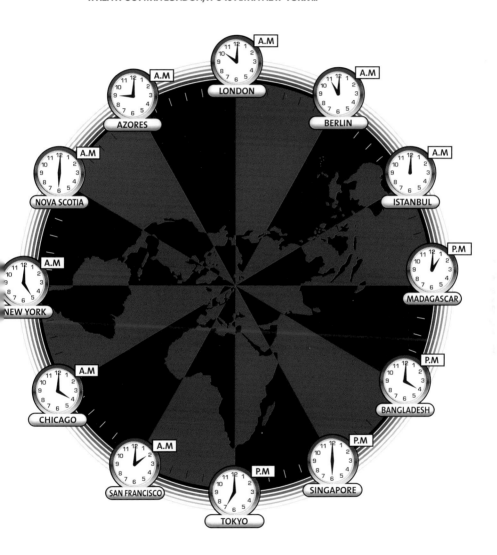

In-flight meals

In-flight meals are an established ritual that some passengers like to denigrate. However, many airlines now provide very good meals in-flight, and if nothing else they help to break up the monotony of a long-haul trip.

Count-down to meal-time

Two months before a flight, companies inform their suppliers of the meals (snacks, lunches, dinners) they wish to serve, but it's only three days in advance that the orders are actually given. Four hours before embarkation, the trays are ready and waiting in the cold room; two hours later, they are placed on trolleys in refrigerated lorries before being loaded on board, where they are stored in the galley kitchens of the various classes. If the flight is long enough to require two meals during the flight, the trolleys are kept chilled with dry ice.

THE COST OF YOUR MEAL
On long-haul flights a meal in economy class is worth between £4 and £8.50, between £21 and £28 in business class and more than £42 in first class (the vintage wines served on board can double the bill). Japanese meals can cost on average 25 per cent more in each class.

ASK FOR THE MENU
Nearly 80 special different kinds of menu can be provided on planes. If you have to follow a special diet, it couldn't be simpler: just notify the company at least 48 hours before departure. The most commonly requested special meals are: vegetarian, kosher, halal, wholefood, fat-free, salt-free and sugar-free.

GETTING THE COFFEE RIGHT ...
DON'T LET IT GRIND YOU DOWN
Coffee is a bit of a headache for airlines. It is the most commonly requested drink on board but every nation has its own way of drinking it. In the United States they like it 'light', weak in northern Europe, high roast in South America, espresso in southern Europe, and flavoured in Asia. It's a multiplicity of taste but, happily, airlines have been pushed into serving better coffee as a result.

FIND OUT

THE AEROPLANE HAS FIRED THE IMAGINATION OF MANY A WRITER
AND ARTIST, BUT IT IS ALSO THE SOURCE OF MANY FEARS.
HOWEVER, FEAR OF FLYING CAN BE OVERCOME – YOU JUST HAVE TO
KNOW HOW. HOW DO YOU FIGHT BACK IF YOU HAVE BEEN A VICTIM OF
OVERBOOKING OR GO ABOUT TRACING YOUR LOST LUGGAGE?
HERE'S SOME ADVICE TO HELP YOUR TRIP GO SMOOTHLY.

Writers between heaven and earth

Symbolising freedom and action, air travel has inspired many writers, who are fascinated by the extraordinary adventure of conquering the sky. Aeroplanes, now an everyday means of transport, also figure in some different tales ...

'Flying for Philip Swallow is essentially a dramatic performance ...'

Philip Swallow has, in fact, flown before; but so seldom, and at such long intervals, that on each occasion he suffers the same trauma, an alternating current of fear and reassurance that charges and relaxes his system in a persistent and exhausting rhythm. While he is on the ground, preparing for his journey, he thinks of flying with exhilaration – soaring up, up and away into the blue empyrean, cradled in aircraft that seem, from a distance, effortlessly at home in that element, as though sculpted from the sky itself. This confidence begins to fade a little when he arrives at the airport and winces at the shrill screaming of jet engines. In the sky the planes look very small. On the runways they look very big. Therefore close up they should look even bigger – but in fact they don't. His own plane, for instance, just outside the window of the assembly lounge, doesn't look quite big enough for all the people who are going to get into it. This impression is confirmed when he passes though the tunnel into the cabin of the aircraft, a cramped tube full of writhing limbs. But when he, and the other passengers, are seated, well-being returns. The seats are so remarkably comfortable that one feels quite content to stay put, but it is reassuring that the aisle is free should one wish to walk up it. There is soothing music playing. The lighting is restful. A stewardess offers him the morning paper. His baggage is safely stowed away in the plane somewhere, or if it is not, that isn't his fault, which is the main thing. Flying is, after all, the only way to travel.

But as the plane taxies to the runway, he makes the mistake of looking out of the window at the wings bouncing gently up and down. The panels and rivets are almost painfully visible, the painted markings weathered, there are streaks of soot on the engine cowlings. It is borne upon him that he is, after all, entrusting his life to a machine, the work of human hands, fallible and subject to decay. And so it goes on, even after the plane has climbed safely into the sky: periods of confidence and pleasure punctuated by spasms of panic and emptiness.

The sang-froid of his fellow passengers is a constant source of wonderment to him, and he observes their deportment carefully. Flying for Philip Swallow is essentially a dramatic performance, and he approaches it like a game amateur actor determined to hold his own in the company of word-perfect professionals.'

Extract from *Changing Places*, David Lodge, Penguin Books

'Things were going to get hot between Gaberone and Maseru ...'

'I left Gaberone for Maseru on board a regular flight of Lesotho Airways, on a DC-3 obviously rented from a South African company. All the notices were written in two languages, and as for the staff, you had the impression that they would have been much happier speaking Afrikaans than English. Just as we were about to take off, when there were only eight passengers on board, a ninth was seen to appear, breathless, on the tarmac, and the co-pilot having cursed 'Damn! Here comes another one', merely flung open the door, which on a DC-3 happens to be at the back of the fuselage and almost at ground level, and scooped up the late arrival. The pilot and co-pilot were almost contemporaries of the Red Baron, or of those air aces at the first air meeting described by Faulkner in *Pylon*. The air hostess was hardly any younger, but much larger, and very nice, rather in the style of a Pomeranian nanny, but accompanied all her announcements with an ironic smirk which seemed to disqualify everything she said, or at least make it seem less important. 'I'm telling you to fasten your seat belts, but actually you can just do what you want.' All in all, the decrepitude of this plane with its crew of facetious fossils, made an excellent impression on me. For one thing, there might be only one DC-3 left in service in the world, all the others having crashed, and you would still not be able to persuade me that this was not the toughest and therefore the most unbreakable plane that had ever been invented. The pilot being as ancient as the plane led you to believe that they had established links of intimacy and connivance, which protected the passengers from any unpleasant surprise. So, for example, if one of the engines failed, the pilot would of course instantly get out of the window with his tool box to repair or change the faulty part, holding on with one hand to the leading edge of the wing, grumbling the while as he had when he had told us 'things will get hot between Gaberone and Maseru'. From the plane, the delicate colours of South Africa – faded pink, linden green and cinder grey – appeared like an oleander hawk moth which had faded in the sun in a shop window.

Extract from *The Front Line*, Jean Rolin, Petite Bibliothèque Payot/Voyageurs

A soaring of the imagination: the plane in art and design

The *Planescape* by Erro'

Erro', an Icelandic 'pop-artist', gathers planes together on a giant canvas, to form a sort of landscape of objects, like a vast collection of random images in a warehouse. As Erro' himself says: 'I usually paint "scapes" in one go, then I go back to them after leaving them for a while, in order to check them and touch up some areas. After painting for so many years, there are certain things I do automatically, which allows me more freedom. At the same time the subconscious corrects and destroys what is being painted. Which makes for some amazing surprises ...'

British Artists

From images of war, such as Robert Taylor's acclaimed paintings of Battle of Britain scenes, to modern airliners, like Anthony Cowland's portrayal of a British Airways Boeing 777, the field of aviation has inspired many artists, not least in Britain. Bristol-born John Young has been painting for over 50 years and has 45 of his works displayed in the RAF Museum at Hendon. He says: 'In aviation the painter has a challenge which can outlast a lifetime.' Robert Taylor, another British painter, has featured in many television programmes, newspaper and magazine articles, and in 1987 his one-man exhibition at the Washington Smithsonian National Air and Space Museum was seen by 10 million visitors.

Aeropittura

In the tradition of futurism, the manifesto of Aeropittura was put together in 1929 by a collective of Italian painters, including Filippo Tommaso Marinetti. This group promoted plastic arts expressing the experience of flight, with the idea of it spreading into the other arts, creating aerosculpture, aeromusic and aeropoetry. The ideology, which was rooted in technology, developed a dynamic aesthetic that explored the idea of leaving the earth behind and studying the relationship between the art of the painter and the movement of planes.

Painted aeroplanes

Now that aeroplanes have got close to technical perfection, the focus is on the potential for artistic creation. Will the skies of tomorrow become a huge art gallery, an exhibition space beyond the reach of most people's imaginations?

Utopia: 'Paint me a plane!'

When in 1997 British Airways decided to abandon the Union Flag and paint the tailfins of its planes in the colours of the world, it sent a shock wave through the world of aviation. It was presented as a revolution in marketing, but Operation Utopia was also a great challenge that co-ordinated the work of 50 artists from around the world. Previously, airlines had only rarely entrusted the decoration of their planes to artists: in 1973 Braniff had requested Calder to paint a DC-3, with the aim of strengthening its links with South America. In the case of the Utopia project, the original idea was to paint all 250 British Airways craft, but following the reaction of some British clients, who were dismayed at the dropping of the national flag, the company abandoned the Utopia project and only half the fleet were decorated. Now the Concorde design, a variation on the Union Flag will slowly appear across all fleets.

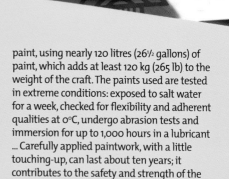

More than a simple decoration

Light colours are preferred to cover the majority of the plane as they reflect away the sun's rays and reduce the temperature in the cabin. In addition to being a well-prepared and polished coating, the paint on an aeroplane is also a defence against corrosion. The first coat is sprayed on, then the top coat is applied with a brush. The surface area of a standard Airbus is equivalent to six tennis courts, and can take more than two weeks to paint, using nearly 120 litres (26½ gallons) of paint, which adds at least 120 kg (265 lb) to the weight of the craft. The paints used are tested in extreme conditions: exposed to salt water for a week, checked for flexibility and adherent qualities at 0°C, undergo abrasion tests and immersion for up to 1,000 hours in a lubricant ... Carefully applied paintwork, with a little touching-up, can last about ten years; it contributes to the safety and strength of the aircraft.

Other decorative projects ...

The Australian company Qantas had two of its craft painted in a style inspired by traditional aboriginal art eight years ago.

The Japanese company All Nippon Airways has had one of its aeroplanes painted with pictures inspired by the Pokémon cartoons. However, this may not be such a smart move given the fleeting popularity of children's fads.

The N'Debele lands take to the air

The work of Emily and Martha Masanabo, two sisters from South Africa, whose work has literally taken off. In their village of Wolwekraal, in the N'Debele lands, they paint fantastic brightly coloured frescoes in geometric designs on the walls of houses, echoing the traditional beaded costumes. The talent of the Masanabo sisters has been recognised a very long way from their village, now that some British Airways planes carry their work. Emily and Martha may paint houses in Wolwekraal, but their imagination has literally taken flight.

One of the Masanobo sisters painting a house in South Africa.

The plane of the future is here now!

Aviation projects still make plane manufacturers dream as much as passengers, but they are so costly to undertake that there has to be international co-operation.

The A3XX/A380

A bar with comfortable seating, a massage suite, a jacuzzi and some games machines ... and all at 30,000 feet! Surely this would take the yawn out of the Frankfurt to Singapore flight. This new 'flying world' is the Airbus A3XX, rechristened the A380. The launch of this revolutionary aircraft, the result of a £6.8 billion investment, has been officially confirmed by Airbus Industrie. The first flight is planned for 2004 at the latest. The A380 defies the laws of aerodynamics: it can travel 16,000 km (10,000 miles), transport 650 passengers, weighs 583 tonnes and measures 80 metres (260 ft) in both width and length. But it is its internal architecture that is the most surprising: two decks, one on top of the other, run the whole length of the plane with a lower deck in addition, making three levels in total. The imagination runs riot – will these planes be like flying ocean liners with facilities previously unheard-of in the air or are they more a way of cramming even more passengers on board to keep down prices? There has even been talk of a charter version, with between 800 and 900 seats. Yet there are limits on the A380 – ones imposed by the design of airports. The plane will not be able to land on all the runways in the world, and the terminals will have to cope with a flow of 650 passengers and their luggage in the space of

15 minutes! This is quite a challenge to be met between now and 2005, when it should enter service.

Boeing's 'flying wing'

A seemingly revolutionary plane, the 'flying wing' idea dates back to the 1920s and was used by the US Air Force in their B-2 stealth bomber but has never been used in civil aviation. There is no tail fin: instead rudders are fitted at the tip of each wing and it is powered by three giant jet engines at the rear. The BWB (blended wing-body aircraft) is twice the size of a Jumbo Jet and will seat 800 passengers in the wings, not in the body of the aircraft. There will be virtually no windows, and instead the view outside will be played on video screens in the seat backs. The flying wing will fly at the same height and speed as a Jumbo, but will be far quieter and use far less fuel.

A380

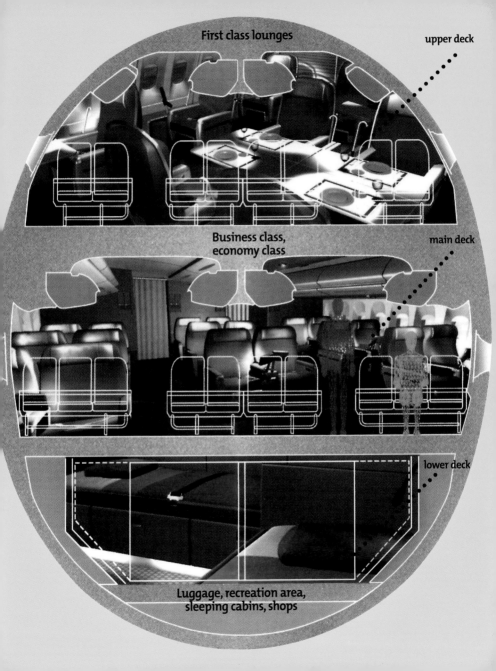

First class lounges

upper deck

Business class,
economy class

main deck

lower deck

Luggage, recreation area,
sleeping cabins, shops

A world away from here ...

Here is some useful information for finding your dream destination.

COUNTRY	DESTINATION (FROM LONDON)
1. AUSTRALIA	Sydney
2. BANGLADESH	Dhaka
3. BARBADOS	Bridgetown
4. BRAZIL	Rio de Janeiro
5. CANADA	Montreal
6. CHINA	Peking
	Hong Kong
7. DENMARK	Copenhagen
8. EGYPT	Cairo
9. FRANCE	Paris
10. GERMANY	Berlin
11. GREECE	Athens
12. INDIA	Mumbai (Bombay)
	Delhi
13. ISRAEL	Tel-Aviv
14. ITALY	Rome
15. JAMAICA	Kingston
16. JAPAN	Tokyo
17. KENYA	Nairobi
18. KOREA	Seoul
19. MAURITIUS	Port Louis
20. MEXICO	Mexico City
21. MOROCCO	Casablanca
	Marrakech
22. NETHERLANDS	Amsterdam
23. NIGERIA	Lagos
24. NORWAY	Oslo
25. POLAND	Warsaw
26. PORTUGAL	Lisbon
27. RUSSIA	Moscow
28. SEYCHELLES	Mahé
29. SOUTH AFRICA	Johannesburg
30. SPAIN	Madrid
31. SWEDEN	Stockholm
32. THAILAND	Bangkok
33. TUNISIA	Tunis
34. TURKEY	Istanbul
35. UNITED STATES	New York
	San Francisco

LENGTH OF FLIGHT (FROM LONDON)	DISTANCE (FROM LONDON)	GMT (W: WINTER, S: SUMMER)	CURRENCY
22 hr 40 min	17,000	W:+10; S:+11	Australian dollar
12 hr 45 min	8,000	+5 hr 30 min	rupee
8 hr 30 min	6,780	−4	Barbados dollar
11 hr 10 min	9,280	W:−3; S:−2	cruzeiro
7 hr 05 min	5,227	W:−5; S:−4	Canadian dollar
9 hr 55 min	8,140	+8	yuan
12 hr 35 min	9,640	+8	Hong Kong dollar
1 hr 50 min	960	W:+1; S:+2	Danish kroner
4 hr 45 min	3,510	W:+2; S:+3	Egyptian pound
1 hr 10 min	340	W:+1; S:+2	French franc
1 hr 45 min	930	W:+1; S:+2	Deutschmark
3 hr 45 min	2,390	W:+2; S:+3	drachma
8 hr 50 min	7,200	+5 hr 30 min	rupee
8 hr 45 min	6,710	+5 hr 30 min	rupee
4 hr 50 min	3,560	W:+2; S:+3	new shekel
2 hr 30 min	1,430	W:+1; S:+2	lira
9 hr 40 min	7,540	−5	Jamaican dollar
11 hr 45 min	9,560	+9	yen
8 hr 35 min	6,820	+3	Kenyan shilling
10 hr 25 min	8,860	+9	won
13 hr 35 min	9,730	+4	rupee
11 hr 50 min	8,950	W:−7; S:−6	peso
2 hr 50 min	2,080	0	diram
3 hr 5 min	2,300	0	diram
1 hr 5 min	360	W:+1; S:+2	guilder
7 hr 20 min	5,020	+1	naira
2 hr	1,150	W:+1; S:+2	Norwegian kroner
2 hr 20 min	1,450	W:+1; S:+2	zloty
2 hr 35 min	1,580	W:0; S:+1	escudo
3 hr 45 min	2,500	W:+3; S:+4	rouble
9 hr 50 min	7,900	+4	rupee
10 hr 50 min	9,070	+2	rand
2 hr 15 min	1,260	W:+1; S:+2	peseta
2 hr 30 min	1,430	W:+1; S:+2	Swedish kroner
11 hr 45 min	9,540	+7	bhat
2 hr	1,820	+1	dinar
3 hr 45 min	2,500	W:+2; S:+3	Turkish lira
7 hr 40 min	5,570	W:−5; S:−4	dollar
10 hr 55 min	8,600	W:−8; S:−7	dollar

Delays and excuses

In 1999 nearly 40 per cent of European flights were more than 15 minutes late, twice as many as in 1992. Where there is a high volume of traffic, the slightest hitch can cause a great deal of disruption.

Delays

Responsibility: the airline

The situation in some airports has become a cause for concern: in Madrid and Milan, for example, one flight in two is late. London Gatwick and Copenhagen come out relatively well, with 21 per cent and 19 per cent of flights delayed respectively. Airlines make the situation worse by neglecting their customer service skills. Lack of waiting areas, lack of staff and overworked staff all conspire to make the lot of the delayed passenger not a happy one. Companies should pay more attention to the problems encountered by delayed passengers and provide facilities (meals and overnight hotel accommodation) free of charge when flights are disrupted. But international regulations are still fairly vague, and not really binding: 'The transporter undertakes to do his best to transport the passenger ... The times shown are not guaranteed'. But the passengers' grumbling is beginning to have an effect. Many of the claims made by passengers with the support of groups like the Air Transport Users Council have led to compensation, sometimes as much as the price of the ticket. 'Delay insurance' is now starting to be offered as part of travel policies, but compensation is low. Woolwich offers £20 for a 12 hour delay with £10 for each extra hour up to a maximum of £120, for instance. Some airline companies offer free air miles to keep their customers quiet.

Charter flights cancelled or delayed

Responsibility: the travel agency or tour operator

This is a difficult point. The situation is mentioned in very small print, vaguely worded, at the end of the sales contract: 'The tour operator reserves the right to change the flight time within the 24 to 48 hours preceding or following the original date.' It is therefore only outside these times that it will recognise responsibility, which is an important detail when it comes to deciding who is responsible for costs when departure is delayed.

70 REASONS FOR DELAY LISTED BY THE IATA

The international air transport association (IATA) lists 70 different reasons for delay: bad weather, technical problems, equipment not available, passenger missing, industrial action, to name but a few. High volume of traffic now features as a regular contributor: after stagnating until the middle of the 1980s, figures have increased by 75 per cent since 1985. The liberalisation of the skies has led to the creation of new companies that have increased air traffic. On the ground and up in the air, jams come at predictable times: busy in the morning and evening, particularly on Fridays and Sundays, and even more in summer.

Law

The rights of passengers

One of the main pieces of legislation covering international air travel is the Warsaw Convention, which was ratified in 1929, which means that the field is wide open for innovation in what is now called 'the rights of the passenger'.

Overbooking and unavailable seats

Responsibility: the company

Overbooking means you're in for a uncomfortable, or even impossible, journey, since several passengers are intent on occupying the same seat! How can this happen? One reason is that, even with the practice of overbooking, many seats can still be left unoccupied on some flights. The scheduled airlines that carry business passengers (the main culprits) put the figure as high as 20 per cent. In order not to fly with empty seats and thus lose money, airlines have started selling up to 120 per cent of the seats available on a plane, thus maximising their profits.

EC Council Regulation 295/91 says that the airline must give you a full refund on your ticket if it is for a scheduled flight, or another flight as soon as possible, or a later flight at a date of your choice, and must compensate you between £100 and £200 depending on the length of flight and how late you are getting to your destination.

Bankruptcy of the carrier or tour operator

Responsibility: the company, the tour operator or the agency

Firms selling air travel legally require an Air Travel Organisers' Licences (ATOL), issued by the CAA, which protects you in the event of company failure. Note that some of the less reputable agents are not licensed by ATOL, so avoid buying tickets through these as you will not be protected. However, if you buy your ticket direct from an airline or receive a scheduled ticket from an agent at the time of payment you are not covered by the ATOL scheme. In these cases you will need insurance that specifically covers airline failure or you may claim from your credit card company if you have paid for the ticket that way.

Lost or stolen ticket

Responsibility: the passenger

You will usually have to buy a new ticket and the price will be refunded to you at the end of the validity period of the lost ticket (normally one year), if you can prove your purchase of the original ticket. You may receive a new ticket free of charge, but will have to sign a form to say that you will pay for it if somebody else uses the lost ticket before it expires.

Passenger cannot take the flight

Responsibility: the passenger

If you cancel or postpone your trip, or you have missed your flight, your rights depend very much on your type of ticket. If you've paid a premium for a full-price ticket, you can take the next plane, ask for a seat from another airline flying to the same destination (the principle of interlining), rebook on another flight, or have your ticket refunded in 30 days. For other tariffs, the conditions for a refund are shown in the contract. Passengers who hold a charter ticket are not able to claim a refund unless they possess cancellation insurance. Check what is covered by the insurance and what reasons for cancellation are accepted. For example 'illness of a close relative' is interpreted very differently in different contracts.

Lost luggage

Reponsibility: the company
You must report the loss of your luggage at the airport of arrival. The airline will then endeavour to track down the lost item – successful in 90 per cent of cases. If, after 21 days, your luggage has not been found it is then considered lost. International regulations provide compensation of £14 per kg (2.2 lb). This isn't a lot, so take out insurance for your luggage if you are taking valuable items with you. Whatever happens, keep your receipts (for insurance) and for the airline company, which may make an *ex gratia* payment.

WHAT SHOULD YOU DO IF THERE IS NO SEAT AVAILABLE?

Some airlines will offer money to passengers willing to give up their seat if they are overbooked. Where there has been overbooking and a passenger cannot fly as a result, the company should compensate the passenger to the value of between £100 and £200 depending on the destination and the length of wait. The passenger may then claim against his travel company to obtain damages. In all cases the company should re-route the passenger as quickly as possible onto another flight. The European directive 295/91 applies only to scheduled flights and does not cover charter flights. In all cases, where there is a long delay, the company (scheduled or charter) should provide for passengers' needs in terms of meals, hotel rooms and so on.

AIR TRAVEL LEGISLATION

EC Directive 295/91, Package Holiday Regulations 1992, The Warsaw Convention 1933, Supply of Goods and Services Act 1982 and the Consumer Protection (Distance Sales) Regulations 2000 are some of the main pieces of legislation applying to air travel.

Calculated risks

Aeroplanes are the safest means of transport in the world. But airlines – the most responsible ones anyway – are making efforts to see that this does not lead to complacency.

The cause of accidents

Human error accounts for the majority of air accidents, at a little over 70 per cent. Far behind come technical faults (9 per cent), failures due to maintenance (6.2 per cent), bad weather (4.1 per cent) and air traffic control problems (3.4 per cent). The remaining 5 per cent are blamed on various events, such as criminal activity.

Landing and take–off

According to a study done at the beginning of the 1990s, nearly 70 per cent of accidents happen on take-off or landing. Descent ranks in third place at 19 per cent, with climbing (7 per cent) and cruising (5 per cent) some way behind.

Checks on personnel

The flight crew changes with every flight. It's unusual for a pilot and co-pilot to work together for several flights in a row. Flight crews are therefore trained in standardised operating procedures. There are regulations preventing staff from flying more than 100 hours a month. When pilots are not flying, they spend time on simulators, practising how to deal with various breakdowns. In addition, pilots may not command a new type of plane without four to five months' training. The hostesses and stewards are also regularly tested and trained.

Aircraft: very closely monitored

An aircraft is regularly checked over, repaired, dismantled and rebuilt. To the extent that after about 20 years, or the equivalent of 50,000 flying hours, it has almost none of its original parts left. Technical faults rarely go unspotted by the technicians. The first stage is routine inspections before and after each flight, supplemented by a more thorough weekly inspection. Then there are more exhaustive monthly and annual inspections, and finally a major inspection after 20,000 flying hours, roughly every four or five years. All these checks amount to about 50,000 hours of work on a Boeing 747.

A new problem: air-rage

The number of violent or disorderly incidents on planes has increased by 50 per cent in the last few years. The major airlines are working hard at finding a way to deal with the problem. It is thought that the ban on smoking, and thus the temptation to replace nicotine with alcohol, has contributed to the problem, in combination with longer flying times. The demystification of plane travel, from a status as a quasi-mythical means of transport to

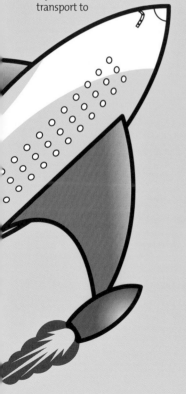

being almost run-of-the-mill, has also been a factor. Crews now have to get tough. If an incident occurs, first of all the heat has to be taken out of the situation by reasoning with the offending passenger. The next step is to tell the culprit that he or she will be met off the plane by police, with the last resort being to divert the plane to the nearest airport to offload the disruptive passenger. Meanwhile the unruly passenger is told to stay in his or her seat, with some companies resorting to handcuffs, others simply using adhesive tape. In response to the increase in these incidents, we could see an international blacklist of dangerous passengers who have had to be restrained.

Airports at risk

The International Federation of Airline Pilots (IFALPA) found 150 airports with significant shortcomings in safety. This is as much to do with the natural surroundings as with staff shortages in the control tower. The most frequently criticised were San Francisco airport, the old airport in Hong Kong, Wellington (New Zealand), the old airport in Oslo, along with Buenos Aires, Caracas, Kabul and Nice.

The risks in figures

There is about one incident per million flights and 700 fatalities per year for 1.5 billion passengers. By way of comparison there are nearly 6,000 deaths on British roads alone, and tens of thousands of people are injured.

Overcoming your fear of flying

The nightmare, the horror, the end of the world ... For some people the mere idea of flying in a plane induces a panic attack, rooting them to the spot and, as often happens, preventing them from boarding a plane. This is quite a handicap, and airlines are helping sufferers to overcome this particular phobia by offering 'fear-of-flying' courses.

Special courses

The course offered by Britannia Airways takes place at East Midlands airport. There are videos and talks by crew members. A senior Britannia training captain explains the basics of flight and the reasons for the noises you hear on an aircraft. Everything is explained in the greatest detail: noises in the cabin, changes in the rhythm of the jet engines on take-off and landing, the raising and lowering of the landing gear, air pockets, wind and lightning. He also reminds you that thanks to the high pressure on the doors there is absolutely no possibility of them opening during flight.

A senior cabin crew member tells you what the training for cabin crew consists of and how the safety of passengers is paramount in everything that takes place on board. A doctor tells you all about fear and phobias and how to overcome them. He is available for a private chat, if you feel it necessary. The crew members then take you on board an aircraft mock-up, used for crew training. It doesn't ever get airborne, but is very realistic, with real aircraft seats, doors and escape slides. After lunch, you will be taken for a flight lasting about an hour to an hour and a half on a Britannia aircraft. The crew members who talked to you will be on the flight as well, to reassure you and to answer any questions you might have.

The course with Britannia costs £130, or £50 if you just want to take the short flight.

Aviatours offer a course at London Heathrow or at Manchester consisting of 'preparation for flight', run by a clinical psychologist, followed by a one hour flight in a Boeing 757 with an experienced British Airways training captain in charge. Parking at the hotel where the course takes place, the course itself, lunch and the flight costs £215. British Airways supports this course, and other airlines have broadly similar courses.

The aim of the talks and the flight is to aid understanding of the functioning of an aircraft and to make people aware that, in aviation, everything has been thought of and that there is a solution to every problem. And it works! Even if the course participants don't go on to board a plane as easily as they get on a bike, they all say that their journeys have become a lot easier. Whatever happens, they can make themselves known to the crew, who will give them a special welcome.

TO FIND OUT MORE
Aviatours: 01252 793250
Britannia: Airways 01582 424155
Virgin Atlantic: 01293 448440

Further reading

Dawood, Dr Richard. *Travellers' Health*, OUP 1992.
How to stay healthy abroad and tips for aircraft health and comfort.

Sabbach, Karl. *21st Century Jet* Pan
Enthralling description of the designing and building of the Boeing 777. If you are at all nervous, you should be put at ease by the incredible amount of work that goes into building an aircraft.

Yaffe, Maurice. *Take the Fear out of Flying* Constable Robinson
Eases fears by fully explaining aviation and offers relaxation exercises.

Health Advice for Travellers A free booklet from the Department of Health.
Information on inoculations, health precautions and how to get form E111 to reclaim medical costs for treatment in EU countries. Available from your local Post Office or call 0800 55577.

Stewart, Stanley. *Flying the Big Jets*, Airlife 2001
An airline captain explains modern flight and takes you on a trip from London to Boston in a Boeing 777.

Getting to Heathrow and Gatwick

HEATHROW

BY TRAIN:
Heathrow Express is the quickest method, departing London Paddington every 15 minutes, which is also how long the journey takes. Tickets can be bought by phone (0845 600 1515) and on the web (www.heathrowexpress.co.uk), and prices start from £20 return.

BY TUBE:
The Piccadilly Line serves all Heathrow terminals; a single ticket is £3?60 but the journey takes nearly an hour. Trains every few minutes from central London.

BY BUS:
The A2 Airbus departs London King's Cross four times an hour and takes over an hour to get to Heathrow, stopping off at various point along the way. A single ticket costs £7.

PARKING:
There is a short stay car park for each of the four terminals. Prices range from £1.80 for 30 minutes to £36 for 24 hours.

Spaces in the long stay car park cost from £12.70 a day. Phone 0800 844844 to book a place.

Business parking rates, for stays of up to three days, are also available.

GATWICK

BY TRAIN:
The quickest service is the Gatwick Express, departing London Victoria four times an hour and taking 30 minutes. Phone 08705 30 15 30 for tickets or book online at www.gatwickexpress.co.uk. A return ticket is £20.

There are other, usually slower services from other London stations and locations around the country.

Bus services to Gatwick are run by a number of operators; ring 0870 574 7777 for details.

PARKING:
Short stay car parking starts at £1.70 for 30 minutes and rises to £16.80 for 24 hours.

Spaces in the long stay car park cost from £6.25 a day. Phone 0800 844844 to book a place.

Useful telephone numbers

AIRPORTS

www.baa.co.uk

HEATHROW
All information
0870 000 0123

GATWICK
Passenger information
01293 535353
Lost Property
(North Terminal)
01293 502013
Lost Property
(South Terminal)
01293 502014

LONDON CITY
020 7646 0000

LUTON
01582 405100

STANSTED
00870 000 0303
Lost property
01279 663293

BIRMINGHAM
0121 767 5511

BRISTOL
01275 474444

CARDIFF
01446 711 111

EAST MIDLANDS
01332 852852

HUMBERSIDE
01652 688456

LEEDS BRADFORD
0113 250 9696

LIVERPOOL
0151 288 4000

MANCHESTER
0161 489 3000

NEWCASTLE
0191 2860966

EDINBURGH
0131 333 1000

GLASGOW
0141 887 1111

BELFAST ALDERGROVE
028 94 484848

DUBLIN
0353 1 18141 111

AIRLINES

AER LINGUS
0645 737747
www.aerlingus.com

AIR CANADA
0990 247226
www.aircanada.ca

AIR FRANCE
0345 581393
www.airfrance.com

AIR INDIA
01753 684828
www.allindia.com

AIR NEW ZEALAND
020 8741 2299
www.airnz.co.nz

AIR UK
0345 666777
www.airuk.co.uk

ALITALIA
020 7602 7111
www.alitalia.it

AMERICAN AIRLINES
0345 789789
www.americanair.com

BRITISH AIRWAYS
0845 773 3377
www.british-airways.com

BRITISH MIDLAND
0845 2407056
www.britishmidland.com

CATHAY PACIFIC
0345 581581
www.cathaypacific.com

CONTINENTAL AIRLINES
0800 776464
www.continental.com

DELTA AIRLINES
0800 414767
www.delta-air.com

EASYJET
0870 6 000 000
www.easyjet.co.uk

EMIRATES
020 7930 3711
www.ekgroup.com

IBERIA
020 7830 0011
www.iberia.es

JAL
020 7408 1000
www.jal.co.jp

KLM
020 8750 9000
www.klm.com

LOGANAIR
01703 651 119
www.loganair.co.uk

LUFTHANSA
0345 737747
www.lufthansa.com

MALAYSIAN AIRLINE SYSTEM
020 8740 2626

QANTAS
0345 747767
www.qantas.com.au

ROYAL AIR MAROC
020 7439 4361
www.royalairmaroc.com

RYANAIR
020 7435 7101
www.ryanair.ie

SABENA
0345 581291
www.sabena.com

SAS
020 7734 4020
www.sas.se

SINGAPORE AIRLINES
020 8747 0007
www.singaporeair.com

SOUTH AFRICAN AIRWAYS
020 7734 9841
www.saa.co.za

SWISSAIR
020 7439 4144
www.swissair.com

TAP AIR PORTUGAL
020 7828 0262
www.Tap.pt

THAI AIRWAYS
020 7499 9113
www.thaiair.com

UNITED AIRLINES
0800 888555
www.ual.com

VARIG
020 7287 3131
www.varig.com

VIRGIN ATLANTIC
01293 747747
www.virgin-atlantic.com

Useful addresses and Internet sites

OFFICIAL ORGANISATIONS

ATUC
Air Transport Users Council

This organisation will give consumer advice between 2 and 5p.m. Mon-Fri on problems with air travel. Write with queries to: ATUC, CAA House, 45-59 Kingsway, London WC2B 6TE

020 7240 6061
www.atuc.

NORTHERN IRELAND
General Consumer Council for Northern Ireland,
Elizabeth House, 116 Hollywood Road, Belfast BT4 1NY

01232 672488

ABTA
Association of British Travel Agents
If you have a dispute with a tour operator or a travel agent and they are members of ABTA contact:

ABTA, 68-71 Newman Street, London W1T 3AH

020 7637 2444

AITO
Association of British Tour Operators
If you have a dispute with a tour operator or a travel agent and they are members of AITO contact:

AITO, 133a St Margret's Road, Twickenham, Middx. TW1 1RG

020 8744 9280

CUSTOMS INFORMATION
Your Yellow Pages will have telephone numbers for your local Customs and Excise Office under the entry 'Government Offices'.

www.hmce.gov.uk

PASSPORT OFFICE HELPLINE
0870 521 0410

OFFICE OF FAIR TRADING
For general consumer advice as well as advice on air travel
08457 22 44 99
www.oft.gov.uk

IATA
IThe site for IATA, the official organisation which includes 260 scheduled airline companies throughout the world.

www.iata.org

THE FOREIGN OFFICE
To find out more about high-risk countries before departure, contact the Foreign Office Travel Advice Unit, Consular Division, Old Admiralty Building, London SW1A 2AF

020 7008 0232/0233
www.fco.org.uk

INTERNET TRAVEL SITES
Travel Finder is a site with links to numerous useful other travel sites, containing information.

www.travel-finder.com/hotsites.htm

A US site with interesting articles and links. It deals with global travel from a US point of view.

www.travel-library.com

The world of travel as seen by Microsoft. The best site for information and sales in travel.

www.expedia.com

Get advice on travel insurance from the Association of British Travel Insurers.

www.abi.org.uk

Practical information on health for travellers: before, during and after your trip.

www.doh.gov.uk/traveladvice/index.htm

Health information, advice and help on global travel from the BBC.

www.bbc.co.uk/health/travel

A magazine with information for the older traveller.

www.saga.co.uk

Features on and ideas for more unusual travel destinations.

www.travelmag.co.uk

Travel articles, photography and ideas.

www.wanderlust.co.uk

SITES FOR BUYING TICKETS
www.accesstravel.8m.com
www.airnet.co.uk
www.cheapflights.co.uk
www.cheaptickets.com
www.ebookers.com
www.flightline.co.uk
www.flights4less.co.uk
www.lastminute.com
www.onlinetravelshop.com
www.travellersweb.ws
www.travelocity.co.uk
www.travelprice.com
www.webworld.co.uk/mall/Arrowguide

VARIOUS

ORGANISATIONS FOR THE DISAABLED
Disabled Living Foundation,
380-384 Harrow Road, London W9 2HU.

020 7289 6111
Produces Flying High - a practical guide to air travel for elderly people and people with disabilities.

ROYAL ASSOCIATION FOR DISABILITY AND REHABILITATION (RADAR)
12 City Forum, 250 City Road, London EC1V 8AF

Produces Access to Air Travel - a guide for people with Reduced Mobility.

020 7250 3222

VACCINATIONS
British Airways Travel Clinics
There are over 30 of these in the UK. Call 01276 685 040 for the nearest one to you.

MASTA
Medical Advisory Services for Travellers Abroad
run the database used by British Airways on what health precautions are need in which country. If you want more information from them call 0906 822 4100. (Calls are charged at 60p per minute.)

YOUR GENERAL PRACTITIONER
Many GPs are authorised to give all vaccinations. He or she will need advance warning to order the vaccine.

INFORMATION ON UK AIRPORTS
www.baa.co.uk

Glossary

AIR SHUTTLE

Routes that are served by a large number of frequent flights, usually hourly or half-hourly. British Airways currently runs shuttle services from London Heathrow: to Belfast, Edinburgh, Glasgow and Manchester.

AIRPORT TAXES

All airports levy a tax on each passenger. Sometimes it is included in the ticket price, sometimes it has to be paid at check-in, usually in local currency or in dollars.

ALLOTMENT

Commitment to reserve a specific number of plane seats, often negotiated yearly between an airline company and a tour operator.

AREA RADIO NAVIGATION

A system of ground radio stations that transmit signals that aircraft equipment can then use to find their position.

BACK-TO-BACK TICKET

A pricing technique whereby two low-price return tickets are bought and the outward and return halves swapped in order to avoid the restrictions on those tickets. Allows substantial savings on flights taken on a regular basis.

BOARDING PASS

Document allowing a passenger to board a plane. It normally shows the seat number. In practice it is the only proof that a passenger has flown on a particular flight with a particular company.

DIRECT FLIGHT

Flight from point A to point B with one or more stops, but without changing planes.

EURO-BUDGET OR EURO-CHALLENGE TARIFFS

Tariffs that apply on European lines and have just one restriction: you must make the outward and return journey with the same carrier.

EXCURSION TARIFF

Low-price ticket, usually requiring both booking and payment to be made at the same time. Flights can be changed, but refunds are not possible.

FREQUENT FLYER PROGRAM

See Loyalty scheme.

GDS

Global distribution systems. The global systems of distribution were set up by the airline companies. They offer universal access to all aeroplane seats and ticket prices. The information is unbiased. Their international nature is also shown in the internationalisation of their service and its diversity (plane tickets, hotel rooms, car hire, cinema and theatre seats).

GPS

Global Positioning System. Equipment that uses a large number of orbiting satellites to navigate with.

HOLIDAY TARIFF

Similar to excursion tariff. Flights can be changed but the ticket is not refundable.

HUB

Airport for changing planes. It is a crossroads for an airline company which will time the arrival of its flights to allow changes to be made as quickly as possible. Heathrow and Gatwick are the main hubs for British Airways.

IATA

International Air Transport Association. It has 250 companies as members and is the official voice for airline companies, fixing the fares for all routes.

INS

Inertial Navigation System. Equipment using gyroscopes and computers to navigate an aircraft.

INTERLINING

According to IATA's rules, its member airlines must accept a ticket issued by another carrier for an equivalent value over an identical route.

LOW-COST AIRLINES

Airline companies that do not provide all the services of a scheduled company but concentrate on only one basic service: carrying the passenger at the lowest cost.

LOYALTY SCHEME

A scheme introduced by airlines to keep their customers loyal. If they travel with the same company, the passenger collects points, with which they can eventually claim free tickets.

MACH

The Mach number is the relationship between the speed of the plane and the local speed of sound, which varies according to the temperature and, as a result, the altitude.

MULTIPLE RESERVATION

A practice that consists of reserving seats on several flights for the same person on the same date. Very popular with business travellers on European flights. See also Overbooking.

NO-SHOW

A passenger who does not turn up at the time of his or her reservation.

NON-STOP FLIGHT

A flight that goes from A to B without a stop-over.

OPEN TICKET

This is a ticket that has no fixed date of return. Full-price tickets are always open.

OPEN JAW

Ticket allowing passenger to arrive in one town and leave from another. For example, arriving in San Francisco and departing from Los Angeles.

OVERBOOKING

Selling more tickets than there are seats available. All airlines use over–booking in anticipation of no-shows

PAX

A passenger in airline-speak.

SLOT

A window of time during which an airline is authorised to land at or take off from an airport.

STAND-BY

A passenger who does not have a fixed reservation on a flight and who goes onto a waiting list.

STICKER

This is fixed to a flight coupon. On an open ticket it shows the flight reserved; on a ticket in use, it shows re-routing.

TOUR OPERATOR

A company that buys in services to put together holidays sold by agencies. Some tour operators sell their own holidays.

TRANSIT

A stop at an airport where a change of plane is required, either with the same company (in line) or with another company (interline).

WAYPOINT

Position co-ordinates inserted into navigational equipment to which aircraft can then fly.

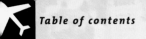

Contents

Fact ≫ 2 – 10

Fun facts and quick quotes

Discover ≫ 11 – 38

Look ≫ 39 – 56

Images of an airport at night